rebel lives **albert einstein** rebel lives **albert einstein** rebel lives

also published in the **rebel lives** series:

Helen Keller, *edited by John Davis*
Haydée Santamaría, *edited by Betsy Maclean*

forthcoming in the **rebel lives** series:

Sacco & Vanzetti, *edited by John Davis*
Louise Michel, *edited by Nic Maclellan*
Tamara "Tania" Bunke, *by Ulises Estrada*

rebel lives, a fresh new series of inexpensive, accessible and provocative books unearthing the rebel histories of some familiar figures and introducing some lesser-known rebels

rebel lives, selections of writings by and about remarkable women and men whose radicalism has been concealed or forgotten. Edited and introduced by activists and researchers around the world, the series presents stirring accounts of race, class and gender rebellion

rebel lives, does not seek to canonize its subjects as perfect political models, visionaries or martyrs but to make available the ideas and stories of imperfect revolutionary human beings to a new generation of readers and aspiring rebels

albert einstein

edited by Jim Green

Ocean Press
Melbourne ■ New York
www.oceanbooks.com.au

ISBN 1-876175-63-X

Library of Congress Catalog Card No: 2003105753

First Printed in Australia 2003

Published by Ocean Press

Australia: GPO Box 3279, Melbourne, Victoria 3001, Australia
Fax: (61-3) 9329 5040 Tel: (61-3) 9326 4280
E-mail: info@oceanbooks.com.au

USA: PO Box 1186, Old Chelsea Stn., New York, NY 10113-1186, USA
Tel: (718) 246-4160

Ocean Press Distributors:

United States and Canada: **Consortium Book Sales and Distribution**
1045 Westgate Drive, Suite 90, Saint Paul, MN 55114-1065, USA
Tel: 1-800-283-3572

Britain and Europe: **Global Book Marketing**
38 King Street, London, WC2E 8JT, UK

Australia and New Zealand: **Palgrave Macmillan**
627 Chapel Street, South Yarra, Victoria, 3141, Australia
E-mail: customer.service@macmillan.com.au

Cuba and Latin America: **Ocean Press**
Calle 21 #406, Vedado, Havana, Cuba

www.oceanbooks.com.au

contents

part five: Jews and Humanism

part six: Capitalism and Socialism

resources

Albert Einstein was declared "Person of the Century" in the December 31, 1999 edition of *Time* magazine. Einstein's accomplishments in the field of theoretical physics were stressed; he was, according to *Time's* Frederic Golden, "the embodiment of pure intellect," "unfathomably profound — the genius among geniuses."

Time's managing editor Walter Isaacson put Einstein's scientific accomplishments in a social context. For Isaacson: "If you had to describe the century's geopolitics in one sentence, it could be a short one: Freedom won. Free minds and free markets prevailed over fascism and communism." The explosion of science and technology, Isaacson argued, "helped secure the triumph of freedom by unleashing the power of free minds and free markets." As the most famous scientist of the century — and one of the most gifted — Einstein deserved *Time's* "Person of the Century" accolade. QED.

There is a major flaw in Isaacson's line of reasoning, though we might still agree with his conclusion. Einstein was an outspoken critic of the triumphalism implicit in all the rhetoric of "free minds and free markets." Far from celebrating capitalism's alleged freeing of the mind, Einstein argued in his 1949 essay, *Why Socialism?*, that the "crippling of individuals" is "the worst evil of capitalism" and that the "economic anarchy of capitalist society as it exists today is, in my opinion, the real source of the evil."

The only hint of Einstein's radicalism in the *Time* article is contained in a reference to its sister magazine, *Life*, which in April 1949 listed the 70-year-old Einstein as one of 50 prominent U.S. "dupes and fellow travelers" used as "weapons" by the communists. Frederic Golden deals with Einstein's politics by patronizing him as "well meaning if naive" and "a soft touch for almost any worthy cause." There is no mention in *Time* of the fact that after World War II, Einstein became a prominent target of the anticommunist crusades in the United States, or that he was an "enemy of America," according to no less an authority than U.S. politician and inquisitor Joseph McCarthy.

The real Albert Einstein — left-wing, pacifist, internationalist; "an anti-Nazi, anti-Franco, antiracist, freethinking, foreign, Jewish scientist" (according to author of *The Einstein File,* Fred Jerome) — is far more interesting than the airbrushed, inaccurate versions to be found in corporate media, where the image of a brilliant, absent-minded professor looms large. Einstein was an agitator, more than willing to challenge authority and to support a range of progressive causes — indeed he felt duty bound to do so.

Einstein, Young Scientist

Born into a middle-class family in Germany in 1879, Einstein was educated there and in Switzerland. German schooling left him with an ingrained mistrust of authority, and the more liberal school he attended in Switzerland provided him a sharp counterpoint. Education reform was, in fact, one of the many issues taken up by Einstein in his years as a public figure.

In 1896, Einstein renounced his German citizenship, most likely to avoid military service. He took up Swiss citizenship in 1901, and was excused from Swiss military service because of varicose veins and flat and sweaty feet (to make matters worse, he never wore socks).

In 1903, Einstein married Mileva Maric, a Serb born in Hungary; they had studied together at the Federal Institute of Technology in Zurich. A daughter, Lieserl, was born to the couple in 1902. Lieserl's fate is unknown — it is assumed she was adopted out, or perhaps she died in infancy. A son, Hans Albert, was born in 1904 and another, Eduard, in 1910.

Following his studies Einstein was unable to secure a university position (or full-time work as a secondary school teacher) at the Institute, and in the following two years worked in a number of temporary teaching positions. While working in Bern at the Swiss Patent Office, Einstein was able to spend much of his spare time studying and writing on theoretical physics. Several articles published in 1905 in *Annalen der Physik*, the leading German physics journal, would (some years later) secure his reputation as a ground-breaking physicist. Thanks to Einstein, that year has been compared to both 1543, when Copernicus published *De Revolutionibus Orbium Coelestium*, and 1686, when Newton completed his *Principia*.

Einstein's 1905 papers were followed by a steady stream of published articles — including important advances on relativity theory in 1907 — before he left Bern (and the Patent Office) in 1909 to take up an appointment as professor of theoretical physics at the University of Zurich. From 1911-17 Einstein worked in several research and professorships throughout Europe, taking up the position of director at the Kaiser Wilhelm Institute for Theoretical Physics in October 1917.

World War I

Just four months before German troops invaded Belgium, the Einsteins moved from Zurich to Berlin. Following the invasion, 93 leading German intellectuals, clergymen and artists signed a *Manifesto to the Civilized World* attempting to justify the invasion of Belgium and arguing, more generally, that German militarism was crucial for the protection of German culture. Einstein, at the age of 35, was one of just four scientists to sign a counterstatement — a *Manifesto to Europeans* — arguing against war and for the creation of a League of Europeans "to weld the continent into an organic whole."

During World War I, Einstein joined the Bund Neues Vaterland (New Fatherland League), which sought an end to the war and the establishment of a supranational organization to prevent future wars. The organization distributed literature, made public statements and held meetings, at which Einstein spoke on occasions. In 1916, the league was banned, but continued a clandestine existence until it could again operate publicly a few months before the end of the war.

Einstein of course welcomed the ending of the war and the establishment of a republic in Germany, and spoke at a student council meeting in the Reichstag, warning against a tyranny of the left replacing the tyranny of the right. And, by 1918, Einstein had made it to a Berlin police blacklist of pacifists and radical social democrats, who were required to obtain prior approval from the military command before applying for passports.

World War I was a time of upheaval in Einstein's personal life. He separated from Mileva in 1914 and, later that year, married his cousin Elsa Löwenthal (their affair began in 1912). Löwenthal was a widow with two daughters, Ilse and Margot. Both of Einstein's marriages were punctuated by affairs and adultery on his part. His treatment of Mileva in particular has been widely criticized and more generally his attitudes toward women were far less progressive than might have been expected from someone with such a radical take on other issues.

Yet Einstein's major preoccupation during and after World War I — of far greater importance to him than either his family or political work — was his scientific research. During the war, Einstein extended his work on relativity to complete a general theory of relativity, fundamentally reconceptualizing the relations between space, time, motion, matter and energy.

Albert Einstein rapidly became a household name. In November 1919 alone, the *New York Times* carried 16 articles on relativity and Einstein. The award of the 1921 Nobel Prize for Physics to Einstein secured his status as a scientific superstar — in the eyes of the public as much as for his scientific colleagues. Einstein came to symbolize scientific progress at a time when great things were expected from science and technology, though later, after the U.S. atomic strikes on Japan, Einstein was recast as a tragic figure. But in the 1920s, Einstein did much to popularize relativity during trips to the United States, a number of European countries, Japan, China and Palestine.

part one: Pacifism, Nationalism, Militarism and Fascism

This "rebel lives" anthology begins with a short but explosive note from Einstein, pleading for civilians to refuse to participate in their leaders' criminal wars: *The Pacifist Problem*. Einstein's was a militant pacifism; for him, peace required eternal struggle against warmongers and against the darker side of human nature. He supported conscientious objection to compulsory military service, describing it as a "violent" tactic but nonetheless the best method of fighting militarism. In 1930, while visiting the United States, Einstein made his famous declaration that if two percent of those called up for military service refused to fight, governments would be rendered powerless, since they could never imprison so many people.

Einstein's fame provided many opportunities to comment publicly on political matters — in particular, his opposition to nationalism: "the measles of mankind," and to militarism: a "plague-spot of civilization," as he comments in *The World As I See it*, included here. He was appalled not only by war but by militarism more generally, including forced military service and the inculcation, beginning in schools and through the media, of militaristic and nationalistic ideologies. In addition to frequent public comments in the media, at public meetings and conferences, Einstein lobbied privately, helping to raise money for pacifist organizations, actively supporting a plethora of groups such as War Resisters' International, the Women's International League for Peace and Freedom and the World Peace League.

In *Letter to a Friend of Peace*, included here, he described the armaments industry as "...the hidden evil power behind the nationalism which is rampant everywhere." Corresponding with Sigmund Freud in 1933, Einstein condemned the power-hungry governing political classes of every nation, and the armaments industry. He asked how such "small cliques" were able to control the majority, pointing to their control of the press, schools and "usually the church as well." He questioned how the ruling classes managed to rouse people to "such wild enthusiasm, even to sacrifice their lives," and found this to be one answer:

> General fear and anxiety create hatred and aggressiveness. The adaptation to warlike aims and activities has corrupted the mentality of man; as a result, intelligent, objective and humane thinking has hardly any effect and is even suspected and persecuted as unpatriotic. (*The Menace of Mass Destruction, 1947*)

Central to Einstein's pacifism was the fundamental principle that war can never be humanized, it can only be abolished. Einstein wrote widely on disarmament, and the best way to achieve it; three such essays have been included here (*America and the Disarmament Conference of 1932, The Question of Disarmament, Address to the Student's Disarmament Meeting*). Einstein believed that agreement or debate about the types of arms permissible in war was worthless — and would be betrayed as soon as war began. Disarmament was an all-or-nothing matter. As long as armies exist, political and economic conflict would inevitably lead to war.

Einstein's pacifism was tolerated in Germany during World War I, if only because of his growing scientific reputation. After the war, he was in an increasingly precarious position as an outspoken pacifist, with left-wing, internationalist views and Jewish heritage. His science was rejected as Jewish and Bolshevik (while in the Soviet Union, his science was sometimes characterized as the product of a fast-fading bourgeoisie). In the inter-war years in Germany, Einstein's science lectures were occasionally disrupted by right-wing agitators; public meetings were held attacking relativity (one of which Einstein attended, making quite a spectacle with his wild applause and his bellowing laughter); the Nazi press depicted him as one of the leaders of the "Jewish world conspiracy," and he was subjected to death threats.

In December 1932, the Einsteins left Germany for a working visit to the United States. The following month, Hitler became chancellor of Germany. The Einstein's holiday house on the outskirts of Berlin was raided by Nazis (ostensibly searching for weapons) and seized, his bank account was blocked and there were more rumored threats to Albert's life. The Einsteins did not return to Germany, and in late 1933, Albert, Elsa, Ilse and Margot, and Albert's secretary Helen Dukas, returned from a Europe trip to the United States, where Albert had been offered a position at the newly-created Institute for Advanced Study in Princeton, New Jersey. Einstein's best scientific work was behind him, but he continued with it until the end of his life, becoming distanced from the mainstream of theoretical physics.

Einstein broke on some issues from a strictly pacifist stance, though his motivation was always the goal of peace and justice. His advocacy of an armed supranational organization is a case in point. With the rise of fascism in Germany, he also temporarily abandoned support for conscientious objection to military service and argued for rearmament in Western European countries (see *On Military Service*). In the United States, Einstein began advocating military preparedness by European countries against the threat of fascism, and in particular Nazism. His 1934 article *On Military Service* calls on countries supporting "peaceful progress" — among which Einstein included the United States, the British Empire, France and Russia — to work together to oppose fascism.

Einstein made public his support for the Lincoln Brigade, the U.S. civilians who volunteered to fight fascism in Spain as part of the International Brigades. He criticized the U.S. Government's policy of neutrality in the Spanish Civil War and its embargo on weapons' sales to the antifascist Spanish Government. In September 1942, Einstein wrote in a letter to Frank Kingdon:

> Why did Washington help to strangulate Loyalist Spain? Why has it an official representative in fascist France? Why does it not recognize a French government in exile? Why does it maintain relations with fascist Spain? Why is there no really serious effort to assist Russia in her dire need? [The U.S.] Government is to a large degree controlled by financiers, the mentality of whom is near to the fascist frame of mind. If Hitler were not a lunatic, he could have remained friends with the Western powers.

part two:
Toward A World Government

In 1922, Einstein joined the Committee on Intellectual Cooperation of the League of Nations, and resigned the following year. In his resignation letter (included here as *A Farewell*), Albert wrote that he wished to work with all his might for the establishment of an international authority superior to nation-states, whereas the committee had no such aim. He rejoined, however, in 1924, partly in light of the fact that his earlier resignation was being exploited as a propaganda tool by German national chauvinists. He hoped that the League of Nations would act as a bulwark against nationalism and militarism and as a positive force for international cooperation — though he was to be greatly disappointed by its record.

Einstein believed that the division of the world into competing nation-states was a fundamental cause of war, and advocated the abolition of national armies, combined with a partial surrender of political and legal sovereignty by nation-states in favor of a supranational authority — or world government. In his *Open Letter to the General Assembly of the United Nations*, included here, Einstein outlined his vision for such an authority, whose members would be popularly elected, and which would have the power — including an armed force — to ensure its decisions were carried out. Einstein argued that the substantial surrender of national sovereignty to a supranational authority was not one of a number of options to end war, but the only option. He also advocated the establishment of an international legislative and judicial body to settle every conflict between nations as a "simple way of dealing with the superficial (i.e. administrative) aspect of the problem" of delivering humanity from the menace of war. Superficial and administrative perhaps — but urgent (all the more so in the era of atomic weapons), and inevitable (by negotiation or by imposition from the victor of a future war).

Einstein was alert to the risks that such a supranational authority might pose. In a 1945 article included later in the anthology, *Atomic War or Peace*, he asked:

> Do I fear the tyranny of a world government? Of course I do. But I fear still more the coming of another war or wars. Any government is certain to be evil to some extent. But a world government is preferable to the far greater evil of wars, particularly with their intensified destructiveness.

With the exception of a brief period, in the aftermath of World War II, of mass public support in the West for a supranational authority, Einstein's call fell on deaf ears. Western rulers tended to view world government as a communist plot, and in the Soviet Union it was seen as a facade for western imperialism.

part three:
Weapons of Mass Destruction

In August 1939, just prior to the outbreak of war in Europe, Einstein sent his *Letter to President Roosevelt on Atomic Weapons,* included here. It was conceivable, Einstein wrote, that uranium could be fashioned into "extremely powerful bombs of a new type." He expressed his fear that the Nazi regime may be working on an atomic weapons' program, and urged a speeding up of experimental work on nuclear fission and for closer contact to be maintained between the U.S. Government and the group of physicists working on fission in the United States.

In October 1939, partly due to Einstein's prompting, the President's Advisory Committee on Uranium was formed. Though he continued to urge expansion and greater coordination of atomic weapons' research, Einstein declined an invitation, the following year, to become a member of an expanded committee.

At the end of the war, with the nuclear strikes on Japan, Einstein spoke out against them, arguing that they were unjustified and motivated by U.S.-Soviet politicking. With the benefit of hindsight, he regretted having urged an atomic weapons' program in the United States during the war.

Following the war, Einstein gave strong support to organizations fighting against militarism and atomic weapons in particular. In May 1946, he became chair of the newly-formed Emergency Committee of Atomic Scientists, which was primarily concerned with education on the dangers of atomic weapons and acted as an umbrella and fund-raising group. Funds raised assisted other organizations such as the Federation of American Scientists and activities like the publication of the *Bulletin of the Atomic Scientists.*

In 1955, scientist-philosopher Bertrand Russell approached Einstein, suggesting that a group of scientists be convened to discuss nuclear disarmament and ways in which war could be abolished. The first such meeting was held in July 1957, in Pugwash, Nova Scotia. Shortly before his death in 1955, Einstein was one of 11 scientists, nine of them Nobel laureates, to sign an initial statement — the *Russell-Einstein Manifesto* — calling for the abolition not only of atomic weapons but also of war itself, regardless of the necessary "distasteful limitations of national sovereignty."

For Einstein, the issue of atomic weapons was subordinate to the broader issues of militarism and nationalism. In *Atomic War or Peace*, included here, he wrote: "As long as there are sovereign nations possessing great power, war is inevitable. That is not an attempt to say when it will come, but only that it is sure to come. That was true before the atomic bomb was made. What has changed is the destructiveness of war." Einstein hoped that the added threat of atomic weapons might facilitate his broader objective of establishing a supranational authority, and wanted the "secret" of the atomic bomb to be monopolized by such an authority (see *A Message to Intellectuals*).

Einstein wanted the U.S. Government to agree to supranational authority over atomic weapons. He did not advocate unilateral nuclear disarmament by the United States, but he wanted the United States to renounce the use of atomic weapons pending the creation of a supranational authority or if supranational control was not achieved.

Though it is possible that the serious pursuit of an atomic weapons' program in the United States might have been delayed if not for Einstein's urgings, the impact of his letters to Roosevelt has often been overstated. The Manhattan Project — large-scale, coordinated work on atomic weapons — did not begin until late 1941, and Einstein himself was blacklisted from the project by U.S. security agencies. He did do some consultancy work on high explosives for the U.S. Navy during the war years, but this work was unrelated to atomic weapons. There is no truth to the widespread view that Einstein's scientific research led to, or provided the foundations for, the development of atomic weapons (see *On the Abolition of the Threat of War*).

On February 12, 1950, Einstein appeared on an NBC network program called "Today With Mrs. Roosevelt," discussing the U.S. Government's plans to build hydrogen bombs far more powerful than the fission bombs dropped on Hiroshima and Nagasaki. Einstein's speech on the program, included here as *National Security,* was typically punchy, warning that the "idea of achieving security through national armament is… a disastrous illusion," that the arms race between the United States and the Soviet Union had assumed a "hysterical character," and that with the advent of hydrogen bombs, "radioactive poisoning of the atmosphere and hence annihilation of any life on Earth has been brought within the range of technical possibilities."

part four:
Human Rights and Civil Rights

Einstein's activities were monitored by U.S. security agencies from his arrival in 1933 until his death. Einstein was forthright in his support for the rights of African Americans (see both *Minorities* and *The Negro Question*), and this, in addition to his pacifism, his internationalism, his socialism and his Jewish heritage, cast him as a subversive in the eyes of U.S. security agencies. Among other acts of solidarity, he joined a committee in defense of the nine "Scottsboro Boys" who were falsely accused of rape; he spoke at the Lincoln University (for black men); he accepted an offer from famous singer and socialist Paul Robeson to co-chair the American Crusade to End Lynching, inviting Robeson to visit him in 1952 (by which time the latter was a prime target of McCarthyism); and he lent support to the National Association for the Advancement of Colored People (NAACP).

The U.S. State Department wanted to block Einstein's visa in late 1932, having received a wad of unsubstantiated allegations from the far-right Woman Patriot Corporation and its vocal president, Mrs. Randolph Frothingham. Not even Stalin himself, Mrs. Frothingham insisted, was affiliated with so many anarcho-communist groups as Einstein. Fearing ridicule and condemnation for blocking Einstein's visit, the State Department issued the visa. Nevertheless, the Federal Bureau of Intelligence — with generous support from numerous other government agencies — continued to monitor him and the FBI file on Einstein grew to over 1,800 pages, listing dozens of "subversive" organizations Einstein supported and in some cases joined.

Einstein railed against bans on "subversive" scientists (and others) from visiting the United States; he argued for clemency for Julius and Ethel Rosenberg, executed in 1953 as spies; he protested the arrest of Communist Party leaders in the United States (*see Human Rights*). His mail was monitored, his phone tapped, his home and office searched and his trash examined.

Einstein's comments on the 1950 NBC program "Today With Mrs. Roosevelt," attracted not only newspaper headlines but also the attention of FBI Director J. Edgar Hoover, who promptly issued a memo to FBI offices across the country seeking all available "derogatory information" on Einstein. Within a few days, Hoover received a large compilation of material listing the "subversive" organizations which Einstein had (allegedly) joined or supported. Yet publicly connecting Einstein to such organizations was more likely to raise their profile and popularity than to lessen his.

Over the next few years, a sustained effort was made to link Einstein to Soviet espionage. Jerome explains: "In Einstein's case... Hoover had no shortage of leads. During the early spy-hunt months of 1950, a slew of accusations linking Einstein to Soviet spy operations arrived at FBI headquarters. And while allegations are not evidence, if it had been anyone but Einstein, the FBI chief would have had him subpoenaed and grilled by congressional committees. But Einstein had too much inter-national support and sympathy..." So nervous did Einstein make the security agencies that they went to great lengths to avoid public knowledge of their investigations into him. All sorts of flimsy allegations linking Einstein to the Soviets were pursued — but nothing could be substantiated.

McCarthyism was gathering steam, and as Jerome notes:

> By the end of 1952, the Republicans, under Eisenhower, had recaptured the White House after 20 years, and all signs pointed to an even more conservative and anticommunist period ahead. Joe McCarthy was the most publicized man in America and seemed to be on an unstoppable power trip — who could predict how far he might rise? More than a hundred officials of the U.S. Communist Party were in jail under the Smith Act, and many states were enforcing their own anticommunist and sedition laws.

Einstein was headline news (again) after publicly urging people to refuse to testify before the House Committee on Un-American Activities in 1953. Einstein had written a letter to high-school teacher William Frauenglass in Brooklyn, included here as *Modern Inquisitional Methods* and first published in the *New York Times* on June 12, 1953. Frauenglass had been called to testify before a Senate sub-committee, but had refused. Einstein's letter attacked "reactionary politicians [who] have managed to instill suspicion of all intellectual efforts in the public by dangling before their eyes a danger from without." It accused them of "proceeding to suppress the freedom of teaching and to deprive of their positions all those who do not prove submissive..." It argued that intellectuals should refuse to testify before the growing number of political committees designed to root out so-called subversives.

Einstein's letter provoked a furious reaction from McCarthy and from the conservative and liberal media alike. Nor was his stance without risks, as Fred Jerome explains: "Hard as it may be today to imagine that a U.S. Government would even consider jailing the world's most famous scientist (at 73, and in failing health), such fears were not irrational. Hoover's repeated [threat to intern] 'communists' in 'detention camps' in the event of a war, had been headlined across the country. And remember that only two years earlier, world-celebrated historian W.E.B. Du Bois was arrested and brought to court in handcuffs — at the age of 83."

The battle against McCarthyism was one of Einstein's last; he fought it vigorously, courageously, and with some success.

part five:
Jews and Humanism

In his early years Einstein did not identify as a Jew; this grew from the increasingly virulent anti-Semitism he witnessed (and was himself subjected to) after he returned to Germany in 1914. He identified with Jews not as a religious but as a cultural grouping with a shared history and a common commitment to social justice and intellectual achievement (the establishment of a Hebrew University in Jerusalem was one of his special causes). In *The Calling of The Jews* and *The Goal of Human Existence*, Einstein delves into the Jewish traditions of humanism and spiritualism, reflecting a truly inclusive worldview: "We should always be aware of the fact that these spiritual values are and always have been the common goal of all humanity."

Two essays by Einstein on the Warsaw Ghetto have been included here: *To the Heroes of the Battle of the Warsaw Ghetto* and *Before the Monument to the Martyred Jews of the Warsaw Ghetto*. In the first, written in the midst of World War II and dedicated to the Jewish resistance fighters of the ghetto, Einstein wrote: "We [Jews] strive to be one in our suffering and in the effort to achieve a better human society."

In response to escalated anti-Semitism following World War I, Einstein became a strong supporter of Zionism. He hoped the settlement of Jews in Palestine would free them from persecution and allow Jewish culture to flourish (to the benefit of Jews and non-Jews alike). He did not support the creation of a separate Jewish state, believing it to be unnecessary and because of his broader opposition to nationalism. Instead, as he wrote in *Our Debt to Zionism*, included here, he wanted peaceful coexistence — and shared political power — between Jews and Arabs in Palestine. He placed much of the blame on the failure to achieve a peaceful coexistence between Arabs and Jews in an undivided Palestine on the divide-and-conquer tactics of the British Mandatory Power, as he argues in *The Jews of Israel*, included here.

Before and during World War II, Einstein expended much time and energy helping Jews fleeing from Nazism, and even though the creation of a Jewish state had not been Einstein's preference, he supported the state of Israel once it was formed. The fate of Jews under fascism was significant in the forming of this opinion; as Einstein argued in *The War is Won But Peace is Not*, included here, Jews had with six million dead been "pushed at the head of the queue [of refugees needing shelter] of Nazi victims, much against their will."

part six:
Capitalism and Socialism

Einstein was a consistent advocate of greater regulation of industry. In his Berlin years, he argued a liberal-reformist position for greater state regulation of industry; later, he argued for a planned, socialist economy.

Einstein became more supportive of socialism as the years passed... and more critical of Stalinism. His opinion of the Soviet Union varied, asserting at times that the jury was still out on the Soviet experiment. He never visited the Soviet Union, in part because of the possibility that such a visit would be used for political advantage by his hosts.

Einstein's 1949 article *Why Socialism?*, published in the first edition of the Marxist journal *Monthly Review* and included here, is his clearest statement in support of a socialist economy. He denounced "the economic anarchy" and "crippling egotism" of capitalism, arguing that the "predatory" nature of capitalist competition leads to unemployment, poverty, economic recessions and to the alienation of the individual, and that private ownership of the means of production results in "an oligarchy of private capital, the enormous power of which cannot be effectively checked even by a democratically organized political society." Einstein wrote that he was:

> ...convinced there is only one way to eliminate these grave evils, namely through the establishment of a socialist economy, accompanied by an educational system which would be oriented toward social goals. In such an economy, the means of production are owned by society itself and are utilized in a planned fashion.

Einstein's pacifist convictions did not sit easily with Marxist views on the need for revolutionary overthrow of the bourgeoisie, and he was also gravely concerned with bureaucracy and political authoritarianism, concluding *Why Socialism?* with these words: "The achievement of socialism requires the solution of some extremely difficult sociopolitical problems: how is it possible, in view of the far-reaching centralization of political and economic power, to prevent bureaucracy from becoming all-powerful and overweening? How can the rights of the individual be protected and therewith a democratic counterweight to the power of bureaucracy be assured?"

Complementary to *Why Socialism?*, an earlier Einstein article has been included in which he expressed a different view. In *Thoughts on the World Economic Crisis*, written during the early 1930s, Einstein raised the possibility of a completely planned economy as the "logically simplest but also most daring method" of addressing economic crises. He argued that much would depend on the outcome of the "forced experiment" of planned economics in Russia, and that it would be presumptuous to reach firm conclusions on that experiment. He expressed a preference for reforms to the capitalist system as opposed to its replacement with a planned economy, urging for shorter working hours to eliminate unemployment, and the fixing of minimum wages to ensure purchasing power would keep pace with production.

Einstein, insistent on the role of individuals in shaping society and ever watchful for the darker side of human nature, also described in *On Wealth,* included here, some of his personal feelings regarding capitalism: "Money only appeals to selfishness and irresistibly invites abuse. Can anyone imagine Moses, Jesus or Gandhi armed with the money-bags of Carnegie?"

Einstein's unwavering advocacy of a supranational authority related to his socialist views, and where he generally considered capitalism to be the root cause of (domestic) economic inequalities and injustice, he identified the division of the world into competing nation-states as the root cause of war.

On the question of science in society, Einstein was no more given to technological determinism than to capitalist triumphalism. His general position was that scientific research and technology could be of enormous benefit to humanity, but in the wrong social context that promise would never be fulfilled. In *Science and Society,* included here, Einstein argued that technological development was a significant cause of unemployment and periodic crises in capitalist economic systems; he bemoaned the use of science and scientists to improve the means of warfare; and he argued that modern weapons, combined with mass communications, "have made it possible to place body and soul under bondage to a central authority." And on many occasions, Einstein urged scientists to carefully consider the social and moral implications of their work.

Jim Green, April 2003

1879 Born on March 14 in Ulm, Germany; grows up in Munich.

1894 The Einsteins move from Munich to Italy, Albert follows after dropping out of the Luitpold Gymnasium.

1895 Fails an entry examination for the Federal Institute of Technology (FIT) in Zurich. Moves to attend a secondary school in Aarau, Switzerland.

1896 Graduates from school and enrolls at the FIT in a four-year course for prospective science teachers. Renounces German citizenship (most likely to avoid military service).

1900 Graduates from the FIT as a teacher of mathematics and physics, but fails to secure employment there. Several temporary teaching jobs from 1900-02 and several failed attempts to secure full-time research and teaching work.

1901 Becomes a Swiss citizen. First scientific paper published in *Annalen der Physik*. Begins work on doctoral dissertation at the University of Zurich but withdraws in early 1902.

1902 Provisional appointment as Technical Expert, Third Class, at the Swiss Patent Office in Bern.

1903 Marries Mileva Maric, a Serbian Hungarian classmate at the FIT. The previous year, Mileva had given birth to their daughter, Lieserl, about whom little is known. Mileva and Albert had two further children — Hans Albert in 1904 and Eduard in 1910.

1905 Papers on relativity, the photoelectric effect (light quanta) and Brownian motion published in *Annalen der Physik*. Earns a doctorate from the University of Zurich for a thesis on the determination of molecular dimensions.

1909 Leaves the Swiss Patent Office in Bern to become professor of theoretical physics at the University of Zurich.

1911–12 Works as professor of theoretical physics at the German-language Karl Ferdinand University in Prague.

1912–14 Works as professor of theoretical physics at the FIT in Zurich.

1914 Moves to Berlin to take up a research position with the Prussian Academy of Sciences and a professorship at the University of Berlin. Albert and Mileva separate; she returns to Zurich with their two sons. Signs *Manifesto to Europeans* distancing himself from German militarism. Involved in, or supports, pacifist initiatives and organizations during World War I. Publishes papers on the General Theory of Relativity during the war years.

1917 Becomes physics director at the Kaiser Wilhelm Institute in Berlin (retaining other academic positions).

1919 Divorces Mileva Maric. Marries his cousin Elsa Löwenthal who has two adult daughters by a previous marriage, Ilse and Margot. A solar eclipse provides evidence in support of Einstein's General Theory of Relativity (the bending of light by the sun's gravitational field) — signaling Einstein's rise to public fame. Though science is still his primary focus, he makes many statements and is involved in many political activities in the inter-war years, especially regarding pacifism, Zionism and the advocacy of national disarmament linked to the creation of a supranational authority.

Early to mid-1920s Trips to a number of European countries, Japan, China, United States, Palestine and South America.

1922 Wins the 1921 Nobel Prize in Physics "for his services to Theoretical Physics, and especially for his discovery of the law of the photoelectric effect."

1930–33 Several visits to the United States (especially the California Institute of Technology) and the United Kingdom.

1933 Albert and Elsa are in the United States when Hitler becomes German Chancellor. They travel to Europe but instead of returning to Berlin, they move to the United States where Albert takes up a position at the Institute for Advanced Study, Princeton, New Jersey. Renounces German citizenship (again).

1935 Sails to Bermuda to obtain immigrant status upon re-entry into the United States (his last trip outside the United States). Granted permanent residency in the United States.

1936 Elsa dies after a brief illness.

1939 Writes the first of several letters to U.S. President Franklin D. Roosevelt warning of the possibility of Germany building an atomic bomb and urging U.S. research into atomic weapons.

1940 Becomes a U.S. citizen, retaining Swiss citizenship.

1945 Officially retires from the Institute for Advanced Study at Princeton but maintains links with the institute and continues his research.

1946 Becomes chair of the newly-formed Emergency Committee of Atomic Scientists. Numerous political activities in his final decade: pacifism; in support of the establishment of a supranational authority; in support of Jews and Zionism; against militarism and racism and McCarthyism in the United States.

1952 Is offered presidency of Israel, but declines.

1955 Dies on April 18 in Princeton, following the rupture of long-existing aortic aneurysm.

PART ONE:

Pacifism, Nationalism, Militarism
and Fascism

The Pacifist Problem

Ladies and gentlemen:

I am very glad of this opportunity of saying a few words to you about the problem of pacifism. The course of events in the last few years has once more shown us how little we are justified in leaving the struggle against armaments and against the war spirit to the governments. On the other hand, the formation of large organizations with a large membership can in itself bring us very little nearer to our goal. In my opinion, the best method in this case is the violent one — conscientious objection, which must be aided by organizations that give moral and material support to the courageous conscientious objectors in each country. In this way we may succeed in making the problem of pacifism an acute one, a real struggle to which forceful spirits will be attracted. It is an illegal struggle, but a struggle for the true rights of the people against their governments as far as they demand criminal acts of their citizens.

Many who think themselves good pacifists will jibe at this out and out pacifism, on patriotic grounds. Such people are not to be relied on in the hour of crisis, as World War I amply proved.

I am most grateful to you for according me an opportunity to give you my views in person.

(First published 1934)

The World As I See It

How strange is the lot of us mortals! Each of us is here for a brief sojourn; for what purpose he knows not, though he sometimes thinks he senses it. But without deeper reflection one knows from daily life that one exists for other people — first of all for those upon whose smiles and well-being our own happiness is wholly dependent, and then for the many, unknown to us, to whose destinies we are bound by the ties of sympathy. A hundred times every day I remind myself that my inner and outer life are based on the labors of other men, living and dead, and that I must exert myself in order to give in the same measure as I have received and am still receiving. I am strongly drawn to a frugal life and am often oppressively aware that I am engrossing an undue amount of the labor of my fellow men. I regard class distinctions as unjustified and, in the last resort, based on force. I also believe that a simple and unassuming life is good for everybody, physically and mentally.

I do not at all believe in human freedom in the philosophical sense. Everybody acts not only under external compulsion but also in accordance with inner necessity. Schopenhauer's saying, "A man can do what he wants, but not want what he wants," has been a very real inspiration to me since my youth; it has been a continual consolation in the face of life's hardships, my own and others', and an unfailing wellspring of tolerance. This realization mercifully mitigates the easily paralyzing sense of responsibility and prevents us from taking ourselves and other people all too seriously; it is conducive to a view of life which, in particular, gives humor its due.

To inquire after the meaning or object of one's own existence or that of all creatures has always seemed to me absurd from an objective point of view. And yet everybody has certain ideals which determine the direction of his endeavors and his judgments. In this sense I have never looked upon ease and happiness as ends in themselves — this ethical basis I call the ideal of a pigsty. The ideals which have lighted my way, and time after time have given me new courage to face life cheerfully, have been Kindness, Beauty and Truth. Without the sense of kinship with men of like mind, without the occupation with the objective world, the eternally unattainable in the field of art and scientific endeavors, life would have seemed to me empty. The trite objects of human efforts — possessions, outward success, luxury — have always seemed to me contemptible.

My passionate sense of social justice and social responsibility has always contrasted oddly with my pronounced lack of need for direct contact with other human beings and human communities. I am truly a "lone traveler" and have never belonged to my country, my home, my friends, or even my immediate family, with my whole heart; in the face of all these ties, I have never lost a sense of distance and a need for solitude — feelings which increase with the years. One becomes sharply aware, but without regret, of the limits of mutual understanding and consonance with other people. No doubt, such a person loses some of his innocence and unconcern; on the other hand, he is largely independent of the opinions, habits and judgments of his fellows and avoids the temptation to build his inner equilibrium upon such insecure foundations.

My political ideal is democracy. Let every man be respected as an individual and no man idolized. It is an irony of fate that I myself have been the recipient of excessive admiration and reverence from my fellow beings, through no fault, and no merit, of my own. The cause of this may well be the desire, unattainable for many, to understand the few ideas to which I have with my feeble powers attained through ceaseless struggle. I am quite aware that it is necessary for the achievement of the objective of an organization that one man should do the thinking and directing and generally bear the responsibility. But the led must not be coerced, they must be able to choose their leader. An autocratic system of coercion, in my opinion, soon degenerates. For force always attracts men of low morality, and I believe it to be an invariable rule that tyrants of genius are succeeded by scoundrels. For this reason I have always been passionately opposed to systems such as we see in Italy and Russia today. The thing that has brought discredit upon the form of democracy as it exists in Europe today is not to be laid to the door of the democratic principle as such, but to the lack of stability of governments and to the impersonal character of the electoral system. I believe that in this respect the United States has found the right way. They have a president who is elected for a sufficiently long period and has sufficient powers really to exercise his responsibility. What I value, on the other hand, in the German political system is the more extensive provision that it makes for the individual in case of illness or need. The really valuable thing in the pageant of human life seems to me not the political state, but the creative, sentient individual, the personality; it alone creates the noble and the sublime, while the herd as such remains dull in thought and dull in feeling.

This topic brings me to that worst outcrop of herd life, the military system, which I abhor. That a man can take pleasure in marching in fours to the strains of a band is enough to make me despise him. He has only been given his big brain by mistake; unprotected spinal marrow was all he needed. This plague-spot of civilization ought to be abolished with all possible speed. Heroism on command, senseless violence, and all the loathsome nonsense that goes by the name of patriotism — how passionately I hate them! How vile and despicable seems war to me! I would rather be hacked in pieces than take part in such an abominable business. My opinion of the human race is high enough that I believe this bogey would have disappeared long ago, had the sound sense of the peoples not been systematically corrupted by commercial and political interests acting through the schools and the press.

The most beautiful experience we can have is the mysterious. It is the fundamental emotion which stands at the cradle of true art and true science. Whoever does not know it and can no longer wonder, no longer marvel, is as good as dead, and his eyes are dimmed. It was the experience of mystery — even if mixed with fear — that engendered religion. A knowledge of the existence of something we cannot penetrate, our perceptions of the profoundest reason and the most radiant beauty, which only in their most primitive forms are accessible to our minds — it is this knowledge and this emotion that constitute true religiosity; in this sense, and in this alone, I am a deeply religious man. I cannot conceive of a God who rewards and punishes his creatures, or has a will of the kind that we experience in ourselves. Neither can I nor would I want to conceive of an individual who survives his physical death; let feeble souls, from fear or absurd egoism, cherish such thoughts. I am satisfied with the mystery of the eternity of life and with the awareness and a glimpse of the marvelous structure of the existing world, together with the devoted striving to comprehend a portion, be it ever so tiny, of the reason that manifests itself in nature.

(1931)

Letter to a Friend of Peace

The point with which you deal in your letter is one of prime importance. The armament industry is indeed one of the greatest dangers that beset mankind. It is the hidden evil power behind the nationalism which is rampant everywhere...

Possibly something might be gained by nationalization. But it is extremely hard to determine exactly what industries should be included. Should the aircraft industry? And how much of the metal industry and the chemical industry?

As regards the munitions industry and the export of war material, the League of Nations has busied itself for years with efforts to get this loathsome traffic controlled — with what little success, we all know. Last year I asked a well-known U.S. diplomat why Japan was not forced by a commercial boycott to desist from her policy of force. "Our commercial interests are too strong" was the answer. How can one help people who rest satisfied with a statement like that?

You believe that a word from me would suffice to get something done in this sphere? What an illusion! People flatter me as long as I do not get in their way. But if I direct my efforts toward objects which do not suit them, they immediately turn to abuse and calumny in defense of their interests. And the onlookers mostly keep out of the limelight, the cowards! Have you ever tested the civil courage of your countrymen? The silently accepted motto is "Leave it alone and say nothing about it." You may be sure that I shall do everything in my power along the lines you indicate, but nothing can be achieved as directly as you think.

(Published in 1934)

America and the Disarmament Conference of 1932

The Americans of today are filled with the cares arising out of the economic conditions in their own country. The efforts of their responsible leaders are directed primarily to remedying the serious unemployment at home. The sense of being involved in the destiny of the rest of the world, and in particular of the mother country of Europe, is even less strong than in normal times.

But the free play of economic forces will not by itself automatically overcome these difficulties. Regulative measures by the community are needed to bring about a sound distribution of labor and consumer goods among mankind; without this even the people of the richest country suffocate. The fact is that since the amount of work needed to supply everybody's needs has been reduced through the improvement of technical methods, the free play of economic forces no longer produces a state of affairs in which all the available labor can find employment. Deliberate regulation and organization are becoming necessary to make the results of technical progress beneficial to all.

If the economic situation cannot be cleared up without systematic regulation, how much more necessary is such regulation for dealing with the international problems of politics! Few of us still cling to the notion that acts of violence in the shape of wars are either advantageous or worthy of humanity as a method of solving international problems. But we are not consistent enough to make vigorous efforts on behalf of the measures which might prevent war, that savage and unworthy relic of the age of barbarism. It requires some power of reflection to see the issue clearly and a certain courage to serve this great cause resolutely and effectively.

Anybody who really wants to abolish war must resolutely declare himself in favor of his own country's resigning a portion of its sovereignty in favor of international institutions: he must be ready to make his own country amenable, in case of a dispute, to the award of an international court. He must, in the most uncompromising fashion, support disarmament all round, as is actually envisaged in the unfortunate Treaty of Versailles. Unless military and aggressively patriotic education is abolished, we can hope for no progress.

No event of the last few years reflects such disgrace on the leading civilized countries of the world as the failure of all disarmament conferences so far; for this failure is due not only to the intrigues of ambitious and unscrupulous politicians but also to the indifference and slackness of the public in all countries. Unless this is changed we shall destroy all the really valuable achievements of our predecessors.

I believe that the American people are only imperfectly aware of the responsibility which rests with them in this matter.

They no doubt think "Let Europe go to the dogs, if she is destroyed by the quarrelsomeness and wickedness of her inhabitants. The good seed of our [President] Wilson has produced a mighty poor crop in the stony group of Europe. We are strong and safe and in no hurry to mix ourselves up in other people's affairs."

Such an attitude is neither noble nor farsighted. America is partly to blame for the difficulties of Europe. By ruthlessly pressing her claims she is hastening the economic and therewith the moral decline of Europe; she has helped to Balkanize Europe and therefore shares the responsibility for the breakdown of political morality and the growth of that spirit of revenge which feeds on despair. This spirit will not stop short of the gates of America — I had almost said, has not stopped short. Look around, and beware!

The truth can be briefly stated: The Disarmament Conference comes as a final chance, to you no less than to us, of preserving the best that civilized humanity has produced. And it is on you, as the strongest and comparatively soundest among us, that the eyes and hopes of all are focused.

(1932)

The Question of Disarmament

The greatest obstacle to the success of the disarmament plan was the fact that people in general left out of account the chief difficulties of the problem. Most objects are gained by gradual steps: for example, the supersession of absolute monarchy by democracy. Here, however, we are concerned with an objective which cannot be reached step by step.

As long as the possibility of war remains, nations will insist on being as perfectly prepared in a military sense as they can, in order to emerge triumphant from the next war. It will also be impossible to avoid educating the youth in warlike traditions and cultivating narrow national vanity joined to the glorification of the warlike spirit, as long as people have to be prepared for occasions when such a spirit will be needed for the purpose of war. To arm is to give one's voice and make one's preparations, not for peace but for war. Therefore people will not disarm step by step; they will disarm at one blow or not at all.

The accomplishment of such a far-reaching change in the life of nations presupposes a mighty moral effort, a deliberate departure from deeply ingrained tradition. Anyone who is not prepared to make the fate of his country in case of a dispute depend entirely on the decisions of an international court of arbitration, and to enter into a treaty to this effect without reserve, is not really resolved to avoid war. It is a case of all or nothing.

It is undeniable that previous attempts to ensure peace have failed through aiming at inadequate compromises.

Disarmament and security are only to be had in combination. The one guarantee of security is an undertaking by all nations to give effect to the decisions of the international authority.

We stand, therefore, at the parting of the ways. Whether we find the way of peace or continue along the old road of brute force, so unworthy of our civilization, depends on ourselves. On the one side the freedom of the individual and the security of society beckon to us; on the other, slavery for the individual and the annihilation of our civilization threaten us. Our fate will be according to our desserts.

(Published in 1934)

Address to the Students' Disarmament Meeting

Preceding generations have presented us with a highly developed science and technology, a most valuable gift which carries with it possibilities of making our life free and beautiful to an extent such as no previous generation has enjoyed. But this gift also brings with it dangers to our existence as great as any that have ever threatened it.

The destiny of civilized humanity depends more than ever on the moral forces it is capable of generating. Hence the task that confronts our age is certainly no easier than the tasks our immediate predecessors successfully performed.

The necessary supply of food and consumer goods can be produced in far fewer hours of work than formerly. Moreover, the problem of distribution of labor and of manufactured goods has become far more difficult. We all feel that the free play of economic forces, the unregulated and unrestrained pursuit of wealth and power by the individual, no longer leads automatically to a tolerable solution of these problems. Production, labor and distribution need to be organized on a definite plan, in order to prevent the elimination of valuable productive energies and the impoverishment and demoralization of large sections of the population.

If unrestricted sacred egoism leads to dire consequences in economic life, it is still worse as a guide in international relations. The development of mechanical methods of warfare is such that human life will become intolerable if people do not discover before long a way of preventing war. The importance of this object is only equaled by the inadequacy of the attempts hitherto made to attain it.

People seek to minimize the danger by limitation of armaments and restrictive rules for the conduct of war. But war is not a parlor game in which the players obediently stick to the rules. Where life and death are at stake, rules and obligations go by the board. Only the absolute repudiation of all war can be of any use here. The creation of an international court of arbitration is not enough. There must be treaties guaranteeing that the decisions of this court shall be made effective by all the nations acting in concert. Without such a guarantee the nations will never have the courage to disarm seriously.

Suppose, for example, that the U.S., English, German and French governments insisted that the Japanese Government put an immediate stop to their warlike operations in China, under pain of a complete economic boycott. Do you suppose that any Japanese government would be found ready to take the responsibility of plunging its country into the perilous adventure of defying this order? Then why is it not done? Why must every individual and every nation tremble for their existence? Because each seeks his own wretched momentary advantage and refuses to subordinate it to the welfare and prosperity of the community.

That is why I began by telling you that the fate of the human race was more than ever dependent on its moral strength today. The way to a joyful and happy existence is everywhere through renunciation and self-limitation.

Where can the strength for such a process come from? Only from those who have had the chance in their early years to fortify their minds and broaden their outlook through study. Thus we of the older generation look to you and hope that you will strive with all your might and achieve what was denied to us.

(1930)

On Military Service

I stand firmly by the principle that a real solution of the problem of pacifism can be achieved only by the organization of a supranational court of arbitration, which, differing from the present League of Nations in Geneva, would have at its disposal the means of enforcing its decisions. In short, an international court of justice with a permanent military establishment, or better, police force. An excellent expression of this conviction of mine is contained in Lord Davies' book, *Force*, the reading of which I strongly recommend to everyone who is seriously concerned with this fundamental problem of mankind.

Taking as starting point this fundamental conviction, I stand for every measure which appears to me capable of bringing mankind nearer to this goal. Up to a few years ago, the refusal to bear arms by courageous and self-sacrificing people was such a measure; it is no longer — especially in Europe — a means to be recommended. When the Great Powers had nearly equally democratic governments, and when none of these powers founded its future plans on military aggression, the refusal to do military service on the part of a fairly large number of citizens might have induced the governments of these powers to look favorably on international legal arbitration. Moreover, such refusals were apt to educate public opinion to real pacifism. The public came to consider as oppression any pressure brought by the state upon its citizens to force them to fulfill their military obligations, besides considering such pressure unethical from the moral standpoint. Under these circumstances, such refusals worked for the highest good.

Today, however, we are brought face to face with the fact that powerful states make independent opinions in politics impossible for their citizens, and lead their own people into error through the systematic diffusion of false information. At the same time, these states become a menace to the rest of the world by creating military organizations which encompass their entire population. This false information is spread by a muzzled press, a centralized radio service, and school education ruled by an aggressive foreign policy. In states of that description, refusal to perform military service means martyrdom and death for those courageous enough to object. In those states in which citizens still cling to some of their political rights, refusal to do military service means weakening the power of resistance of the remaining sane portions of the civilized world.

Because of this, no reasonable human being would today favor the refusal to do military service, at least not in Europe, which is at present particularly beset with dangers.

I do not believe that under present circumstances passive resistance is an effective method, even if carried out in the most heroic manner. Other times, other means, even if the final aim remains the same.

The confirmed pacifist must therefore at present seek a plan of action different from that of former, more peaceful times. He must try to work for this aim: That those states which favor peaceful progress may come as close together as possible in order to diminish the likelihood that the warlike programs of political adventurers whose states are founded on violence and brigandage will be realized. I have in mind, in the first place, well-considered and permanent concerted action on the part of the United States and the British Empire, together with France and Russia when possible.

Perhaps the present danger will facilitate this rapprochement and thus bring about a pacifistic solution of international problems. This would be the hopeful side to the present dark situation; here consistent action can contribute much toward influencing public opinion in the right direction.

(1934)

PART TWO

Toward A World Goverment

A Farewell
(Letter of Resignation to the German
Secretary of the League of Nations)

Dear Mr. Dufour-Feronce:

Your kind letter must not go unanswered, otherwise you may get a mistaken notion of my attitude. The grounds for my resolve to go to Geneva no more are as follows: experience has, unhappily, taught me that the commission (the Committee on Intellectual Cooperation of the League of Nations), taken as a whole, stands for no serious determination to make real progress in the task of improving international relations. It looks to me far more like an embodiment of the principle *ut aliquid fieri videatur* [urge to intervene, born of impotence]. The commission seems to me even worse in this respect than the League taken as a whole.

It is precisely because I desire to work with all my might for the establishment of an international arbitrating and regulative authority *superior to the state*, and because I have this object so very much at heart, that I feel compelled to leave the commission.

The commission has given its blessing to the oppression of the cultural minorities in all countries by causing a national commission to be set up in each of them, which is to form the only channel of communication between the intellectuals of a country and the commission. It has thereby deliberately abandoned its function of giving moral support to the national minorities in their struggle against cultural oppression.

Further, the attitude of the commission in the matter of combating the chauvinistic and militaristic tendencies of education in the various countries has been so lukewarm that no serious efforts in this fundamentally important sphere can be hoped for from it.

The commission has invariably failed to give moral support to those individuals and associations who have thrown themselves without reserve into the task of working for an international order and against the military system.

The commission has never made any attempt to resist the appointment of members whom it knew to stand for tendencies the very reverse of those they were bound in duty to advance.

I will not bother you with any further arguments, since you will understand my resolve well enough from these few hints. It is not my business to draw up an indictment but merely to explain my position. If I nourished any hope whatever I should act differently — of that you may be sure.

(1923)

Open Letter to the General Assembly of the United Nations

We are caught in a situation in which every citizen of every country, his children, and his life's work, are threatened by the terrible insecurity which reigns in our world today. The progress of technological development has not increased the stability and the welfare of humanity. Because of our inability to solve the problem of international organization, it has actually contributed to the dangers which threaten peace and the very existence of mankind.

The delegates of 55 governments, meeting in the second General Assembly of the United Nations, undoubtedly will be aware of the fact that during the last two years — since the victory over the Axis powers — no appreciable progress has been made either toward the prevention of war or toward agreement in specific fields such as control of atomic energy and economic cooperation in the reconstruction of war-devastated areas.

The United Nations cannot be blamed for these failures. No international organization can be stronger than the constitutional powers given it, or than its component parts want it to be. As a matter of fact, the United Nations is an extremely important and useful institution *provided* the peoples and governments of the world realize that it is merely a transitional system toward the final goal, which is the establishment of a supranational authority vested with sufficient legislative and executive powers to keep the peace. The present impasse lies in the fact that there is no sufficient, reliable supranational authority. Thus the responsible leaders of all governments are obliged to act on the assumption of eventual war. Every step motivated by that assumption contributes to the general fear and distrust and hastens the final catastrophe. However strong national armaments may be, they do not create military security for any nation nor do they guarantee the maintenance of peace.

There can never be complete agreement on international control and the administration of atomic energy or on general disarmament until there is a modification of the traditional concept of national sovereignty. For as long as atomic energy and armaments are considered a vital part of national security no nation will give more than lip service to international treaties. Security is indivisible. It can be reached only when necessary guarantees of law and enforcement are obtained everywhere, so that military security is no longer the problem of any single state. There is no compromise possible between preparation for war, on the one hand, and preparation of a world society based on law and order on the other.

Every citizen must make up his mind. If he accepts the premise of war, he must reconcile himself to the maintenance of troops in strategic areas like Austria and Korea; to the sending of troops to Greece and Bulgaria; to the accumulation of stockpiles of uranium by whatever means; to universal military training; to the progressive limitation of civil liberties. Above all, he must endure the consequences of military secrecy which is one of the worst scourges of our time and one of the greatest obstacles to cultural betterment.

If on the other hand every citizen realizes that the only guarantee for security and peace in this atomic age is the constant development of a supranational government, then he will do everything in his power to strengthen the United Nations. It seems to me that every reasonable and responsible citizen in the world must know where his choice lies.

Yet the world at large finds itself in a vicious circle since the UN powers seem to be incapable of making up their minds on this score. The Eastern and Western blocs each attempt frantically to strengthen their respective power positions. Universal military training, Russian troops in Eastern Europe, U.S. control over the Pacific Islands, even the stiffening colonial policies of the Netherlands, Great Britain and France, atomic and military secrecy — are all part of the old familiar jockeying for position.

The time has come for the United Nations to strengthen its moral authority by bold decisions. First, the authority of the General Assembly must be increased so that the Security Council as well as all other bodies of the United Nations will be subordinated to it. As long as there is a conflict of authority between the assembly and the Security Council, the effectiveness of the whole institution will remain necessarily impaired.

Second, the method of representation at the United Nations should be considerably modified. The present method of selection by government appointment does not leave any real freedom to the appointee. Furthermore, selection by governments cannot give the peoples of the world the feeling of being fairly and proportionately represented. The moral authority of the United Nations would be considerably enhanced if the delegates were elected directly by the people. Were they responsible to an electorate, they would have much more freedom to follow their consciences. Thus we could hope for more statesmen and fewer diplomats.

Third, the General Assembly should remain in session throughout the critical period of transition. By staying constantly on the job, the assembly could fulfill two major tasks: first, it could take the initiative toward the establishment of a supranational order; second, it could take quick and effective steps in all those danger areas (such as currently exist on the Greek border) where peace is threatened.

The assembly, in view of these high tasks, should not delegate its powers to the Security Council, especially while that body is paralyzed by the shortcomings of the veto provisions. As the only body competent to take the initiative boldly and resolutely, the United Nations must act with utmost speed to create the necessary conditions for international security by laying the foundations for a real world government.

Of course there will be opposition. It is by no means certain that the Soviet Union — which is often represented as the main antagonist to the idea of world government — would maintain its opposition if an equitable offer providing for real security were made. Even assuming that the Soviet Union is now opposed to the idea of world government, once she becomes convinced that world government is nonetheless in the making her whole attitude may change. She may then insist on only the necessary guarantees of equality before the law so as to avoid finding herself in perennial minority as in the present Security Council.

Nevertheless, we must assume that despite all efforts the Soviet Union and her allies may still find it advisable to stay out of such a world government. In that case — and only after all efforts have been made in utmost sincerity to obtain the cooperation of Russia and her allies — the other countries would have to proceed alone. It is of the utmost importance that this partial world government be very strong, comprising at least two-thirds of the major industrial and economic areas of the world. Such strength in itself would make it possible for the partial world government to abandon military secrecy and all the other practices born of insecurity.

Such a partial world government should make it clear from the beginning that its doors remain wide open to any nonmember — particularly Russia — for participation on the basis of complete equality. In my opinion, the partial world government should accept the presence of observers from nonmember governments at all its meetings and constitutional conventions.

In order to achieve the final aim — which is one world, and not two hostile worlds — such a partial world government must never act as an alliance against the rest of the world. The only real step toward world government is world government itself.

In a world government the ideological differences between the various component parts are of no grave consequence. I am convinced that the present difficulties between the United States and the Soviet Union are not due primarily to ideological differences. Of course, these ideological differences are a contributing element in an already serious tension. But I am convinced that even if the United States and Russia were both capitalist countries — or communist, or monarchist, for that matter — their rivalries, conflicting interests and jealousies would result in strains similar to those existing between the two countries today.

The United Nations now and world government eventually must serve one single goal — the guarantee of the security, tranquillity and the welfare of all mankind.

(1947)

PART THREE

Weapons of Mass Destruction

Letter to President Roosevelt on Atomic Weapons

F.D. Roosevelt
President of the United States
White House
Washington, D.C.

August 2, 1939

Sir:

Some recent work by E. Fermi and L. Szilard, which has been communicated to me in manuscript, leads me to expect that the element uranium may be turned into a new and important source of energy in the immediate future.

Certain aspects of the situation which has arisen seem to call for watchfulness and, if necessary, quick action on the part of the [U.S.] Administration. I believe therefore that it is my duty to bring to your attention the following facts and recommendations:

In the course of the last four months it has been made probable through the work of Joliot in France as well as Fermi and Szilard in the United States — that it may become possible to set up a nuclear chain reaction in a large mass of uranium, by which vast amounts of power and large quantities of new radium-like elements would be generated. Now it appears almost certain that this could be achieved in the immediate future.

This new phenomenon would also lead to the construction of bombs, and it is conceivable — though much less certain — that extremely powerful bombs of a new type may thus be constructed. A single bomb of this type, carried by boat and exploded in a port, might very well destroy the whole port together with some of the surrounding territory. However, such bombs might very well prove to be too heavy for transportation by air.

The United States has only very poor ores of uranium in moderate quantities. There is some good ore in Canada and the former Czechoslovakia, while the most important source of uranium is in the Belgian Congo.

In view of the situation you may think it desirable to have more permanent contact maintained between the administration and the group of physicists working on chain reactions in the United States. One possible way of achieving this might be for you to entrust with this task a person who has your confidence and who could perhaps serve in an unofficial capacity. His task might comprise the following:

a) to approach government departments, keep them informed of the further developments, and put forward recommendations for government action, giving particular attention to the problem of securing a supply of uranium ore for the United States;

b) to speed up the experimental work, which is at present being carried on within the limits of the budgets of university laboratories, by providing funds, if such funds be required, through his contacts with private persons who are willing to make contributions for this cause, and perhaps also by obtaining the cooperation of industrial laboratories which have the necessary equipment.

I understand that Germany has actually stopped the sale of uranium from the Czechoslovakian mines she has taken over. That she should have taken such early action might perhaps be understood on the ground that the son of the German Under Secretary of State, von Weizsäcker, is attached to the Kaiser Wilhelm Institute in Berlin where some of the U.S. work on uranium is now being repeated.

Yours very truly,
Albert Einstein

(1939)

Atomic War or Peace

The release of atomic energy has not created a new problem. It has merely made more urgent the necessity of solving an existing one. One could say that it has affected us quantitatively, not qualitatively. As long as there are sovereign nations possessing great power, war is inevitable. That is not an attempt to say when it will come, but only that it is sure to come. That was true before the atomic bomb was made. What has been changed is the destructiveness of war.

I do not believe that civilization will be wiped out in a war fought with the atomic bomb. Perhaps two-thirds of the people of the Earth might be killed. But enough men capable of thinking, and enough books, would be left to start again, and civilization could be restored.

I do not believe that the secret of the bomb should be given to the United Nations. I do not believe it should be given to the Soviet Union. Either course would be like a man with capital, wishing another man to work with him on some enterprise, and starting out by simply giving that man half of his money. The other man might choose to start a rival enterprise, when what is wanted is his cooperation. The secret of the bomb should be committed to a world government, and the United States should immediately announce its readiness to give it to a world government. This government should be founded by the United States, the Soviet Union and Great Britain, the only three powers with great military strength. All three of them should commit to this world government all of their military strength. The fact that there are only three nations with great military power should make it easier, rather than harder, to establish such a government.

Since the United States and Great Britain have the secret of the atomic bomb and the Soviet Union does not, they should invite the Soviet Union to prepare and present the first draft of a constitution of the proposed world government. That will help dispel the distrust of the Russians, which they already feel because the bomb is being kept a secret chiefly to prevent their having it. Obviously the first draft would not be the final one, but the Russians should be made to feel that the world government will assure them their security.

It would be wise if this constitution were to be negotiated by a single American, a single Briton and a single Russian. They would have to have advisers, but these advisers should only advise when asked. I believe three men can succeed in writing a workable constitution acceptable to them all. Six or seven men, or more, probably would fail. After the three great powers have drafted a constitution and adopted it, the smaller nations should be invited to join the world government. They should be free to stay out, and though they should feel perfectly secure in staying out, I am sure they would wish to join. Naturally they should be entitled to propose changes in the constitution as drafted by the Big Three. But the Big Three should go ahead and organize the world government, whether the smaller nations join or not.

The power of this world government would be over all military matters, and there need be only one further power. That is to interfere in countries where a minority is oppressing a majority, and so is creating the kind of instability that leads to war. Conditions such as exist in Argentina and Spain should be dealt with. There must be an end to the concept of nonintervention, for to end it is part of keeping the peace.

The establishment of this world government must not have to wait until the same conditions of freedom are to be found in all three of the great powers. While it is true that in the Soviet Union the minority rules, I do not consider that internal conditions there are of themselves a threat to world peace. One must bear in mind that the people in the Soviet Union did not have a long political education, and changes to improve Russian conditions had to be carried through by a minority for the reason that there was no majority capable of doing it. If I had been born a Russian, I believe I could have adjusted myself to this situation.

It should not be necessary, in establishing a world government with a monopoly of military authority, to change the structure of the three Great Powers. It would be for the three individuals who draft the constitution to devise ways for their different structures to be fitted together for collaboration.

Do I fear the tyranny of a world government? Of course I do. But I fear still more the coming of another war or wars. Any government is certain to be evil to some extent. But a world government is preferable to the far greater evil of wars, particularly with their intensified destructiveness. If such a world government is not established by a process of agreement, I believe it will come anyway, and in a much more dangerous form. For war or wars will end in one power being supreme and dominating the rest of the world by its overwhelming military strength.

Now we have the atomic secret, we must not lose it, and that is what we should risk doing, if we give it to the United Nations or to the Soviet Union. But we must make it clear as quickly as possible that we are not keeping the bomb a secret for the sake of our power, but in the hope of establishing peace through a world government, and we will do our utmost to bring this world government into being.

I appreciate that there are people who favor a gradual approach to world government, even though they approve of it as the ultimate objective. The trouble with taking little steps, one at a time, in the hope of reaching the ultimate goal, is that while they are being taken, we continue to keep the bomb without making our reason convincing to those who do not have it. That of itself creates fear and suspicion, with the consequence that the relations of rival sovereignties deteriorate dangerously. So while people who take only a step at a time may think they are approaching world peace, they actually are contributing by their slow pace to the coming of war. We have no time to spend in this way. If war is to be averted, it must be done quickly.

We shall not have the secret very long. I know it is argued that no other country has money enough to spend on the development of the atomic bomb, which assures us the secret for a long time. It is a mistake often made in this country to measure things by the amount of money they cost. But other countries which have the materials and the men and care to apply them to the work of developing atomic power can do so, for men and materials and the decision to use them, and not money, are all that are needed.

I do not consider myself the father of the release of atomic energy. My part in it was quite indirect. I did not, in fact, foresee that it would be released in my time. I believed only that it was theoretically possible. It became practical through the accidental discovery of chain reaction, and this was not something I could have predicted. It was discovered by Hahn in Berlin, and he himself misinterpreted what he discovered. It was Lize Meitner who provided the correct interpretation, and escaped from Germany to place the information in the hands of Niels Bohr.

I do not believe that a great era of atomic science is to be assured by organizing science, in the way large corporations are organized. One can organize to apply a discovery already made, but not to make one. Only a free individual can make a discovery. There can be a kind of organizing by which scientists are assured their freedom and proper conditions of work. Professors of science in U.S. universities, for instance, should be relieved of some of their teaching so as to have time for more research. Can you imagine an organization of scientists making the discoveries of Charles Darwin?

Nor do I believe that the vast private corporations of the United States are suitable to the needs of these times. If a visitor should come to this country from another planet, would he not find it strange that in this country so much power is permitted to private corporations without their having commensurate responsibility? I say this to stress that the U.S. Government must keep the control of atomic energy, not because socialism is necessarily desirable, but because atomic energy was developed by the government, and it would be unthinkable to turn over this property of the people to any individuals or groups of individuals. As to socialism, unless it is international to the extent of producing world government which controls all military power, it might more easily lead to wars than capitalism, because it represents a still greater concentration of power.

To give any estimate when atomic energy can be applied to constructive purposes is impossible. What now is known is only how to use a fairly large quantity of uranium. The use of small quantities, sufficient, say, to operate a car or an airplane, so far is impossible, and one cannot predict when it will be achieved. No doubt, it will be achieved, but nobody can say when. Nor can one predict when materials more common than uranium can be used to supply atomic energy. Presumably all materials used for this purpose will be among the heavier elements of high atomic weight. Those elements are relatively scarce due to their lesser stability. Most of these materials may have already disappeared by radioactive disintegration. So though the release of atomic energy can be, and no doubt will be, a great boon to mankind, that may not be for some time.

I myself do not have the gift of explanation with which I am able to persuade large numbers of people of the urgency of the problems the human race now faces. Hence I should like to commend someone who has this gift of explanation, Emery Reves, whose book, *The Anatomy of the Peace,* is intelligent, *read* clear, brief, and, if I may use the abused term, dynamic on the topic of war and need for world government.

Since I do not foresee that atomic energy is to be a great boon for a long time, I have to say that for the present it is a menace. Perhaps it is well that it should be. It may intimidate the human race to bring order into its international affairs, which, without the pressure of fear, it undoubtedly would not do.

(1945)

A Message to Intellectuals

We meet today, as intellectuals and scholars of many nationalities, with a deep and historic responsibility placed upon us. We have every reason to be grateful to our French and Polish colleagues whose initiative has assembled us here for a momentous objective: to use the influence of wise men in promoting peace and security throughout the world. This is the age-old problem with which Plato, as one of the first, struggled so hard: to apply reason and prudence to the solution of man's problems instead of yielding to atavist instincts and passions.

By painful experience we have learnt that rational thinking does not suffice to solve the problems of our social life. Penetrating research and keen scientific work have often had tragic implications for mankind, producing, on the one hand, inventions which liberated man from exhausting physical labor, making his life easier and richer; but on the other hand, introducing a grave restlessness into his life, making him a slave to his technological environment, and — most catastrophic of all — creating the means for his own mass destruction. This, indeed, is a tragedy of overwhelming poignancy!

However poignant that tragedy is, it is perhaps even more tragic that, while mankind has produced many scholars so extremely successful in the field of science and technology, we have been for a long time so inefficient in finding adequate solutions to the many political conflicts and economic tensions which beset us. No doubt, the antagonism of economic interests within and among nations is largely responsible to a great extent for the dangerous and threatening condition in the world today. Man has not succeeded in developing political and economic forms of organization which would guarantee the peaceful coexistence of the nations of the world. He has not succeeded in building the kind of system which would eliminate the possibility of war and banish forever the murderous instruments of mass destruction.

We scientists, whose tragic destination has been to help in making the methods of annihilation more gruesome and more effective, must consider it our solemn and transcendent duty to do all in our power in preventing these weapons from being used for the brutal purpose for which they were invented. What task could possibly be more important for us? What social aim could be closer to our hearts? That is why this congress has such a vital mission. We are here to take counsel with each other. We must build spiritual and scientific bridges linking the nations of the world. We must overcome the horrible obstacles of national frontiers.

In the smaller entities of community life, man has made some progress toward breaking down antisocial sovereignties. This is true, for example, of life within cities and, to a certain degree, even of society within individual states. In such communities tradition and education have had a moderating influence and have brought about tolerable relations among the peoples living within those confines. But in relations among separate states complete anarchy still prevails. I do not believe that we have made any genuine advance in this area during the last few thousand years. All too frequently conflicts among nations are still being decided by brutal power, by war. The unlimited desire for ever greater power seeks to become active and aggressive wherever and whenever the physical possibility offers itself.

Throughout the ages, this state of anarchy in international affairs has inflicted indescribable suffering and destruction upon mankind; again and again it has depraved the development of men, their souls and their well-being. At times it has almost annihilated whole areas.

However, the desire of nations to be constantly prepared for warfare has, in addition, still other repercussions upon the lives of men. The power of every state over its citizens has grown steadily during the last few hundred years, no less in countries where the power of the state has been exercised wisely, than in those where it has been used for brutal tyranny. The function of the state to maintain peaceful and ordered relations among and between its citizens has become increasingly complicated and extensive largely because of the concentration and centralization of the modern industrial apparatus. In order to protect its citizens from attacks from without a modern state requires a formidable, expanding military establishment. In addition, the state considers it necessary to educate its citizens for the possibilities of war, an "education" not only corrupting to the soul and spirit of the young, but also adversely affecting the mentality of adults. No country can avoid this corruption. It pervades the citizenry even in countries which do not harbor outspoken aggressive tendencies. The state has thus become a modern idol whose suggestive power few men are able to escape.

Education for war, however, is a delusion. The technological developments of the last few years have created a completely new military situation. Horrible weapons have been invented, capable of destroying in a few seconds huge masses of human beings and tremendous areas of territory. Since science has not yet found protection from these weapons, the modern state is no longer in a position to prepare adequately for the safety of its citizens.

How, then, shall we be saved?

Mankind can only gain protection against the danger of un-imaginable destruction and wanton annihilation if a supranational organization has alone the authority to produce or possess these weapons. It is unthinkable, however, that nations under existing conditions would hand over such authority to a supranational organization unless the organization would have the legal right and duty to solve all the conflicts which in the past have led to war. The functions of individual states would be to concentrate more or less upon internal affairs; in their relation with other states they would deal only with issues and problems which are in no way conducive to endangering international security.

Unfortunately, there are no indications that governments yet realize that the situation in which mankind finds itself makes the adoption of revolutionary measures a compelling necessity. Our situation is not comparable to anything in the past. It is impossi-ble, therefore, to apply methods and measures which at an earlier age might have been sufficient. We must revolutionize our think-ing, revolutionize our actions, and must have the courage to revolutionize relations among the nations of the world. Clichés of yesterday will no longer do today, and will, no doubt, be hope-lessly out of date tomorrow. To bring this home to men all over the world is the most important and most fateful social function intellectuals have ever had to shoulder. Will they have enough courage to overcome their own national ties to the extent that is necessary to induce the peoples of the world to change their deep-rooted national traditions in a most radical fashion?

A tremendous effort is indispensable. If it fails now, the supra-national organization will be built later, but then it will have to be built upon the ruins of a large part of the now existing world. Let us hope that the abolition of the existing international anarchy will not need to be bought by a self-inflicted world catastrophe the dimensions of which none of us can possibly imagine. The time is terribly short. We must act now if we are to act at all.

(1948)

On the Abolition of the Threat of War

My part in producing the atomic bomb consisted in a single act: I signed a letter to President Roosevelt, pressing the need for experiments on a large scale in order to explore the possibilities for the production of an atomic bomb.

I was fully aware of the terrible danger to mankind in case this attempt succeeded. But the likelihood that the Germans were working on the same problem with a chance of succeeding forced me to this step. I could do nothing else although I have always been a convinced pacifist. To my mind, to kill in war is not a whit better than to commit ordinary murder.

As long, however, as the nations are not resolved to abolish war through common actions and to solve their conflicts and protect their interests by peaceful decisions on a legal basis, they feel compelled to prepare for war. They feel obliged to prepare all possible means, even the most detestable ones, so as not to be left behind in the general armament race. This road necessarily leads to war, a war which under the present conditions means universal destruction.

Under these circumstances the fight against *means* has no chance of success. Only the radical abolition of wars and of the threat of war can help. This is what one has to work for. One has to be resolved not to let himself be forced to actions that run counter to this goal. This is a severe demand on an individual who is conscious of his dependence on society. But it is not an impossible demand.

Gandhi, the greatest political genius of our time, has pointed the way. He has shown of what sacrifices people are capable once they have found the right way. His work for the liberation of India is a living testimony to the fact that a will governed by firm conviction is stronger than a seemingly invincible material power.

(1952)

National Security

I am grateful to you, Mrs. Roosevelt, for the opportunity to express my conviction on this most important political question.

The idea of achieving security through national armament is, at the present state of military technique, a disastrous illusion. On the part of the United States, this illusion has been particularly fostered by the fact that this country succeeded first in producing an atomic bomb. The belief seemed to prevail that in the end it would be possible to achieve decisive military superiority. In this way, any potential opponent would be intimidated, and security, so ardently desired by all of us, brought to us and all of humanity. The maxim which we have been following during these last five years has been, in short: security through superior military power, whatever the cost.

This mechanistic, technical-military psychological attitude has had its inevitable consequences. Every single act in foreign policy is governed exclusively by one viewpoint: How do we have to act in order to achieve utmost superiority over the opponent in case of war? Establishing military bases at all possible strategically important points on the globe. Arming and economic strengthening of potential allies. Within the country: concentration of tremendous financial power in the hands of the military; militarization of the youth; close supervision of the loyalty of the citizens, in particular, of the civil servants, by a police force growing more conspicuous every day. Intimidation of people of independent political thinking. Subtle indoctrination of the public by radio, press and schools. Growing restriction of the range of public information under the pressure of military secrecy.

The armament race between the United States and the Soviet Union, originally supposed to be a preventive measure, assumes hysterical character. On both sides, the means to mass destruction are perfected with feverish haste — behind the respective walls of secrecy. The hydrogen bomb appears on the public horizon as a probably attainable goal. Its accelerated development has been solemnly proclaimed by the president. If it is successful, radioactive poisoning of the atmosphere and hence annihilation of any life on Earth has been brought within the range of technical possibilities. The ghostlike character of this development lies in its apparently compulsory trend. Every step appears as the unavoidable consequence of the preceding one. In the end, there beckons more and more clearly general annihilation.

Is there any way out of this impasse created by man himself? All of us, and particularly those who are responsible for the attitude of the United States and the Soviet Union, should realize that we may have vanquished an external enemy, but have been incapable of getting rid of the mentality created by the war. It is impossible to achieve peace as long as every single action is taken with a possible future conflict in view. The leading point of view of all political action should therefore be: what can we do to bring about a peaceful coexistence and even loyal cooperation of the nations? The first problem is to do away with mutual fear and distrust. Solemn renunciation of violence (not only with respect to means of mass destruction) is undoubtedly necessary. Such renunciation, however, can be effective only if at the same time a supranational judicial and executive body is set up empowered to decide questions of immediate concern to the security of the nations. Even a *declaration* of the nations to collaborate loyally in the realization of such a "restricted world government" would considerably reduce the imminent danger of war.

In the last analysis, every kind of peaceful cooperation among men is primarily based on mutual trust and only secondly on institutions such as courts of justice and police. This holds for nations as well as for individuals. And the basis of trust is loyal give and take.

What about international control? Well, it may be of secondary use as a police measure. But it may be wise not to overestimate its importance. The times of Prohibition come to mind and give one pause.

(1950)

PART FOUR:

Human Rights and Civil Rights

Minorities

It seems to be a universal fact that minorities — especially when the individuals composing them can be recognized by physical characteristics — are treated by the majorities among whom they live as an inferior order of beings. The tragedy of such a fate lies not merely in the unfair treatment to which these minorities are automatically subjected in social and economic matters, but also in the fact that under the suggestive influence of the majority most of the victims themselves succumb to the same prejudice and regard their kind as inferior beings. This second and greater part of the evil can be overcome by closer association and by deliberate education of the minority, whose spiritual liberation can thus be accomplished.

The resolute efforts of the American Negroes in this direction deserve approval and assistance.

(Published in 1934)

The Negro Question

I am writing as one who has lived among you in America only a little more than 10 years. And I am writing seriously and warningly. Many readers may ask: "What right has he to speak out about things which concern us alone, and which no newcomer should touch?"

I do not think such a standpoint is justified. One who has grown up in an environment takes much for granted. On the other hand, one who has come to this country as a mature person may have a keen eye for everything peculiar and characteristic. I believe he should speak out freely on what he sees and feels, for by so doing he may perhaps prove himself useful.

What soon makes the new arrival devoted to this country is the democratic trait among the people. I am not thinking here so much of the democratic political constitution of this country, however highly it must be praised. I am thinking of the relationship between individual people and of the attitude they maintain toward one another.

In the United States everyone feels assured of his worth as an individual. No one humbles himself before another person or class. Even the great difference in wealth, the superior power of a few, cannot undermine this healthy self-confidence and natural respect for the dignity of one's fellow man.

There is, however, a somber point in the social outlook of Americans. Their sense of equality and human dignity is mainly limited to men of white skins. Even among these there are prejudices of which I as a Jew am clearly conscious; but they are unimportant in comparison with the attitude of the "Whites" toward their fellow citizens of darker complexion, particularly toward Negroes. The more I feel an American, the more this situation pains me. I can escape the feeling of complicity in it only by speaking out.

Many a sincere person will answer me: "Our attitude toward Negroes is the result of unfavorable experiences which we have had by living side by side with Negroes in this country. They are not our equals in intelligence, sense of responsibility, reliability."

I am firmly convinced that whoever believes this suffers from a fatal misconception. Your ancestors dragged these black people from their homes by force; and in the white man's quest for wealth and an easy life they have been ruthlessly suppressed and exploited, degraded into slavery. The modern prejudice against Negroes is the result of the desire to maintain this unworthy condition.

The ancient Greeks also had slaves. They were not Negroes but white men who had been taken captive in war. There could be no talk of racial differences. And yet Aristotle, one of the great Greek philosophers, declared slaves inferior beings who were justly subdued and deprived of their liberty. It is clear that he was enmeshed in a traditional prejudice from which, despite his extraordinary intellect, he could not free himself.

A large part of our attitude toward things is conditioned by opinions and emotions which we unconsciously absorb as children from our environment. In other words, it is tradition — besides inherited aptitudes and qualities — which makes us what we are. We but rarely reflect how relatively small as compared with the powerful influence of tradition is the influence of our conscious thought upon our conduct and convictions.

It would be foolish to despise tradition. But with our growing self-consciousness and increasing intelligence we must begin to control tradition and assume a critical attitude toward it, if human relations are ever to change for the better. We must try to recognize what in our accepted tradition is damaging to our fate and dignity — and shape our lives accordingly.

I believe that whoever tries to think things through honestly will soon recognize how unworthy and even fatal is the traditional bias against Negroes.

What, however, can the man of good will do to combat this deeply rooted prejudice? He must have the courage to set an example by word and deed, and must watch lest his children become influenced by this racial bias.

I do not believe there is a way in which this deeply entrenched evil can be quickly healed. But until this goal is reached there is no greater satisfaction for a just and well-meaning person than the knowledge that he has devoted his best energies to the service of the good cause.

(1946)

Human Rights

Ladies and Gentlemen:

You are assembled today to devote your attention to the problem of human rights. You have decided to offer me an award on this occasion. When I learned about it, I was somewhat depressed by your decision. For in how unfortunate a state must a community find itself if it cannot produce a more suitable candidate upon whom to confer such a distinction?

In a long life I have devoted all my faculties to reach a somewhat deeper insight into the structure of physical reality. Never have I made any systematic effort to ameliorate the lot of men, to fight injustice and suppression, and to improve the traditional forms of human relations. The only thing I did was this: in long intervals I have expressed an opinion on public issues whenever they appeared to me so bad and unfortunate that silence would have made me feel guilty of complicity.

The existence and validity of human rights are not written in the stars. The ideals concerning the conduct of men toward each other and the desirable structure of the community have been conceived and taught by enlightened individuals in the course of history. Those ideals and convictions which resulted from historical experience, from the craving for beauty and harmony, have been readily accepted in theory by man — and at all times, have been trampled upon by the same people under the pressure of their animal instincts. A large part of history is therefore replete with the struggle for those human rights, an eternal struggle in which a final victory can never be won. But to tire in that struggle would mean the ruin of society.

In talking about human rights today, we are referring primarily to the following demands: protection of the individual against arbitrary infringement by other individuals or by the government; the right to work and to adequate earnings from work; freedom of discussion and teaching; adequate participation of the individual in the formation of his government. *These* human rights are nowadays recognized theoretically, although, by abundant use of formalistic, legal maneuvers, they are being violated to a much greater extent than even a generation ago. There is, however, one other human right which is infrequently mentioned but which seems to be destined to become very important: this is the right, or the duty, of the individual to abstain from cooperating in activities which he considers wrong or pernicious. The first place in this respect must be given to the refusal of military service. I have known instances where individuals of unusual moral strength and integrity have, for that reason, come into conflict with the organs of the state. The Nuremberg Trial of the German war criminals was tacitly based on the recognition of the principle: criminal actions cannot be excused if committed on government orders; conscience supersedes the authority of the law of the state.

The struggle of our own days is being waged primarily for the freedom of political conviction and discussion as well as for the freedom of research and teaching. The fear of communism has led to practices which have become incomprehensible to the rest of civilized mankind and exposed our country to ridicule. How long shall we tolerate that politicians, hungry for power, try to gain political advantages in such a way? Sometimes it seems that people have lost their sense of humor to such a degree that the French saying, "Ridicule kills," has lost its validity.

(1954)

Modern Inquisitional Methods

May 16, 1953

Dear Mr. Frauenglass:

Thank you for your communication. By "remote field" I referred to the foundations of physics.

The problem with which the intellectuals of this country are confronted is very serious. The reactionary politicians have managed to instill suspicion of all intellectual efforts in the public by dangling before their eyes a danger from without.

Having succeeded so far, they are now proceeding to suppress the freedom of teaching and to deprive of their positions all those who do not prove submissive, i.e., to starve them.

What ought the minority of intellectuals to do against this evil? Frankly, I can only see the revolutionary way of noncooperation in the sense of Gandhi's. Every intellectual who is called before one of the committees ought to refuse to testify, i.e., he must be prepared for jail and economic ruin, in short, for the sacrifice of his personal welfare in the interest of the cultural welfare of his country.

However, this refusal to testify must not be based on the well-known subterfuge of invoking the Fifth Amendment against possible self-incrimination, but on the assertion that it is shameful for a blameless citizen to submit to such an inquisition and that this kind of inquisition violates the spirit of the constitution.

If enough people are ready to take this grave step they will be successful. If not, then the intellectuals of this country deserve nothing better than the slavery which is intended for them.

P.S. This letter need not be considered "confidential."

(1953)

PART FIVE

Jews and Humanism

The Calling of the Jews

This is a time when there is a particular need for people of philosophical persuasion — that is to say, friends of wisdom and
truth — to join together. For while it is true that our time has accumulated more knowledge than any earlier age, that love of
truth and insight which lent wings to the spirit of the Renaissance
has grown cold, giving way to sober specialization rooted in the
material spheres of society rather than in the spiritual.

In centuries past Judaism clung exclusively to its moral and
spiritual tradition. Its teachers were its only leaders. But with
adaptation to a larger social whole this spiritual orientation has
receded into the background, though even today the Jewish people owe to it their apparently indestructible vigor. If we are to
preserve that vigor for the benefit of humanity, we must hold to
that spiritual orientation toward life.

The Dance about the Golden Calf was not merely a legendary
episode in the history of our forefathers — an episode that seems
to me in its simplicity more innocent than that total adherence
to material and selfish goals threatening Judaism in our own
days. At this time a union of those who rally to the spiritual

heritage of our people has supreme justification. This is all the more true for a group that is free of all historical and national narrowness. We Jews should be and remain the carriers and patrons of spiritual values. But we should also always be aware of the fact that these spiritual values are and always have been the common goal of all humanity.

(1936)

The Goal of Human Existence

Our age is proud of the progress it has made in man's intellectual development. The search and striving for truth and knowledge is one of the highest of man's qualities — though often the pride is most loudly voiced by those who strive the least. And certainly we should take care not to make the intellect our god; it has, of course, powerful muscles, but no personality. It cannot lead, it can only serve; and it is not fastidious in its choice of a leader. This characteristic is reflected in the qualities of its priests, the intellectuals. The intellect has a sharp eye for methods and tools, but is blind to ends and values. So it is no wonder that this fatal blindness is handed on from old to young and today involves a whole generation.

Our Jewish forbears, the prophets and the old Chinese sages understood and proclaimed that the most important factor in giving shape to our human existence is the setting up and establishment of a goal; the goal being a community of free and happy human beings who by constant inward endeavor strive to liberate themselves from the inheritance of antisocial and destructive instincts. In this effort the intellect can be the most powerful aid. The fruits of intellectual effort, together with the striving itself, in cooperation with the creativity of an artist, lend content and meaning to life.

But today the rude passions of man reign in our world, more unrestrained than ever before. Our Jewish people, a small minority everywhere, with no means of defending themselves by force, are exposed to the cruelest suffering, even to complete annihilation, to a far greater degree than any other people in the world. The hatred raging against us is grounded in the fact that we have upheld the ideal of harmonious partnership and given it expression in word and deed among the best of our people.

(1943)

To the Heroes of the Battle of the Warsaw Ghetto

They fought and died as members of the Jewish nation, in the struggle against organized bands of German murderers. To us these sacrifices are a strengthening of the bond between us, the Jews of all countries. We strive to be one in suffering and in the effort to achieve a better human society, that society which our prophets have so clearly and forcibly set before us as a goal.

The Germans as an entire people are responsible for these mass murders and must be punished as a people if there is justice in the world and if the consciousness of collective responsibility is not to perish from the earth entirely. Behind the Nazi party stands the German people, who elected Hitler after he had in his book and speeches made his shameful intentions clear beyond the possibility of misunderstanding. The Germans are the only people who have not made any serious attempt of counteraction leading to the protection of the innocently persecuted. When they are entirely defeated and begin to lament over their fate, we must not let ourselves be deceived again, but keep in mind that they deliberately used the humanity of others to make preparation for their last and most grievous crime against humanity.

(1944)

Before the Monument to the Martyred Jews of the Warsaw Ghetto

The monument before which you have gathered today was built to stand as a concrete symbol of our grief over the irreparable loss our martyred Jewish nation has suffered. It shall also serve as a reminder for us who have survived to remain loyal to our people and to the moral principles cherished by our fathers. Only through such loyalty may we hope to survive this age of moral decay.

The more cruel the wrong that men commit against an individual or a people, the deeper their hatred and contempt for their victim. Conceit and false pride on the part of a nation prevent the rise of remorse for its crime. Those who have had no part in the crime, however, have no sympathy for the sufferings of the innocent victims of persecution and no awareness of human solidarity. That is why the remnants of European Jewry are languishing in concentration camps and the sparsely populated lands of this earth close their gates against them. Even our right, so solemnly pledged, to a national homeland in Palestine is being betrayed. In this era of moral degradation in which we live the voice of justice no longer has any power over men.

Let us clearly recognize and never forget this: That mutual cooperation and furtherance of living ties between the Jews of all lands is our sole physical and moral protection in the present situation. But for the future our hope lies in overcoming the general moral abasement which today gravely menaces the very existence of humanity. Let us labor with all our powers, however feeble, to the end that humanity recover from its present moral degradation and gain a new vitality and a new strength in its striving for right and justice as well as for a harmonious society.

(1948)

The Jews of Israel

There is no problem of such overwhelming importance to us Jews as consolidating that which has been accomplished in Israel with amazing energy and an unequalled willingness for sacrifice. May the joy and admiration that fill us when we think of all that this small group of energetic and thoughtful people has achieved give us the strength to accept the great responsibility which the present situation has placed upon us.

When appraising the achievement, however, let us not lose sight of the cause to be served by this achievement: rescue of our endangered brethren, dispersed in many lands, by uniting them in Israel; creation of a community which conforms as closely as possible to the ethical ideals of our people as they have been formed in the course of a long history.

One of these ideals is peace, based on understanding and self-restraint, and not on violence. If we are imbued with this ideal, our joy becomes somewhat mingled with sadness, because our relations with the Arabs are far from this ideal at the present time. It may well be that we would have reached this ideal, had we been permitted to work out, undisturbed by others, our relations with our neighbors, for we want peace and we realize that our future development depends on peace.

It was much less our own fault or that of our neighbors than of the Mandatory Power, that we did not achieve an undivided Palestine in which Jews and Arabs would live as equals, free, in peace. If one nation dominates other nations, as was the case in the British Mandate over Palestine, she can hardly avoid following the notorious device of *Divide et Impera*. In plain language this means: create discord among the governed people so they will not unite in order to shake off the yoke imposed upon them. Well, the yoke has been removed, but the seed of dissension has borne fruit and may still do harm for some time to come — let us hope not for too long.

The Jews of Palestine did not fight for political independence for its own sake, but they fought to achieve free immigration for the Jews of many countries where their very existence was in danger; free immigration also for all those who were longing for a life among their own. It is no exaggeration to say that they fought to make possible a sacrifice perhaps unique in history.

I do not speak of the loss in lives and property fighting an opponent who was numerically far superior, nor do I mean the exhausting toil which is the pioneer's lot in a neglected arid country. I am thinking of the additional sacrifice that a population living under such conditions has to make in order to receive, in the course of 18 months, an influx of immigrants which comprise more than one third of the total Jewish population of the country. In order to realize what this means you have only to visualize a comparable feat of the American Jews. Let us assume there were no laws limiting the immigration into the United States; imagine that the Jews of this country volunteered to receive more than one million Jews from other countries in the course of one year and a half, to take care of them, and to integrate them into the economy of this country. This would be a tremendous achievement, but still very far from the achievement of our brethren in Israel. For the United States is a big, fertile country, sparsely populated with a high living standard and a highly developed productive capacity, not to compare with small Jewish Palestine whose inhabitants, even without the additional burden of mass immigration, lead a hard and frugal life, still threatened by enemy attacks. Think of the privations and personal sacrifices which this voluntary act of brotherly love means for the Jews of Israel.

The economic means of the Jewish Community in Israel do not suffice to bring this tremendous enterprise to a successful end. For 100,000 out of more than 300,000 people who immigrated to Israel since May 1948 no homes or work could be made available. They had to be concentrated in improvised camps under conditions which are a disgrace to all of us.

It must not happen that this magnificent work breaks down because the Jews of this country do not help sufficiently or quickly enough. Here, to my mind, is a precious gift with which all Jews have been presented: the opportunity to take an active part in this wonderful task.

(1949)

The War is Won But Peace is Not

Physicists find themselves in a position not unlike that of Alfred Nobel. Alfred Nobel invented the most powerful explosive ever known up to his time, a means of destruction par excellence. In order to atone for this, in order to relieve his human conscience he instituted his awards for the promotion of peace and for achievements of peace. Today, the physicists who participated in forging the most formidable and dangerous weapon of all times are harassed by an equal feeling of responsibility, not to say guilt. And we cannot desist from warning, and warning again, we cannot and should not slacken in our efforts to make the nations of the world, and especially their governments, aware of the unspeakable disaster they are certain to provoke unless they change their attitude toward each other and toward the task of shaping the future. We helped in creating this new weapon in order to prevent the enemies of mankind from achieving it ahead of us, which, given the mentality of the Nazis, would have meant inconceivable destruction and the enslavement of the rest of the world. We delivered this weapon into the hands of the U.S. and British people as trustees of the whole of mankind, as fighters for peace and liberty. But so far we fail to see any guarantee of peace, we do not see any guarantee of the freedoms that were promised to the nations in the Atlantic Charter. The war is won, but the peace is not. The great powers, united in fighting, are now divided over the peace settlements. The world was promised freedom from fear, but in fact fear has increased tremendously since the termination of the war. The world was promised freedom from want, but large parts of the world are faced with starvation while others are living in abundance. The nations were promised liberation and justice. But we have witnessed, and are witnessing even now, the sad spectacle of "liberating" armies firing into populations who want their independence and social equality, and supporting in those countries, by force of arms, such parties and personalities as appear to be most suited to serve vested interests. Territorial questions and arguments of power, obsolete though they are, still prevail over the essential demands of common welfare and justice. Allow me to be more specific about just one case, which is but a symptom of the general situation: the case of my own people, the Jewish people.

As long as Nazi violence was unleashed only, or mainly, against the Jews the rest of the world looked on passively, and even treaties and agreements were made with the patently criminal government of the Third Reich. Later, when Hitler was on the point of taking over Rumania and Hungary, at the time when Maidanek and Oswiecim were in Allied hands, and the methods of the gas chambers were well known all over the world, all attempts to rescue the Rumanian and Hungarian Jews came to naught because the doors of Palestine were closed to Jewish immigrants by the British Government, and no country could be found that would admit those forsaken people. They were left to perish like their brothers and sisters in the occupied countries.

We shall never forget the heroic efforts of the small countries, of the Scandinavian, the Dutch, the Swiss nations, and of individuals in the occupied parts of Europe who did all in their power to protect Jewish lives. We do not forget the humane attitude of the Soviet Union who was the only one among the big powers to open her doors to hundreds of thousands of Jews when the Nazi armies were advancing in Poland. But after all that has happened, and was not prevented from happening, how is it today? While in Europe territories are being distributed without any qualms about the wishes of the people concerned, the remainders of European Jewry, one-fifth of its pre-war population, are again denied access to their haven in Palestine and left to hunger and cold and persisting hostility. There is no country, even today, that would be willing or able to offer them a place where they could live in peace and security. And the fact that many of them are still kept in the degrading conditions of concentration camps by the Allies gives sufficient evidence of the shamefulness and hopelessness of the situation. These people are forbidden to enter Palestine with reference to the principle of democracy, but actually the Western powers, in upholding the ban of the White Paper, are yielding to the threats and the external pressure of five vast and underpopulated Arab states. It is sheer irony when the British Foreign Minister tells the poor lot of European Jews they should remain in Europe because their genius is needed there, and, on the other hand, advises them not to try to get at the head of the queue lest they might incur new hatred and persecution. Well, I am afraid, they cannot help it; with their six million dead they have been pushed at the head of the queue, of the queue of Nazi victims, much against their will.

The picture of our postwar world is not bright. As far as we, the physicists, are concerned, we are no politicians and it has never been our wish to meddle in politics. But we know a few things that the politicians do not know. And we feel the duty to speak up and to remind those responsible that there is no escape into easy comforts, there is no distance ahead for proceeding little by little and delaying the necessary changes into an indefinite future, there is no time left for petty bargaining. The situation calls for a courageous effort, for a radical change in our whole attitude, in the entire political concept. May the spirit that prompted Alfred Nobel to create his great institution, the spirit of trust and confidence, of generosity and brotherhood among men, prevail in the minds of those upon whose decisions our destiny rests. Otherwise human civilization will be doomed.

(1945)

PART SIX

Capitalism and Socialism

Why Socialism?

Is it advisable for one who is not an expert on economic and social issues to express views on the subject of socialism? I believe for a number of reasons that it is.

Let us first consider the question from the point of view of scientific knowledge. It might appear that there are no essential methodological differences between astronomy and economics: scientists in both fields attempt to discover laws of general acceptability for a circumscribed group of phenomena in order to make the interconnection of these phenomena as clearly understandable as possible. But in reality such methodological differences do exist. The discovery of general laws in the field of economics is made difficult by the circumstance that observed economic phenomena are often affected by many factors which are very hard to evaluate separately. In addition, the experience which has accumulated since the beginning of the so-called civilized period of human history has — as is well known — been largely influenced and limited by causes which are by no means exclusively economic in nature. For example, most of the major states of history owed their existence to conquest. The conquering peoples established themselves, legally and economically, as the privileged class of the conquered country. They seized for themselves a monopoly of the land ownership and appointed a priesthood from among their own ranks. The priests, in control of education, made the class division of society into a permanent institution and created a system of values by which the people were thenceforth, to a large extent unconsciously, guided in their social behavior.

But historic tradition is, so to speak, of yesterday; nowhere have we really overcome what Thorstein Veblen called "the predatory phase" of human development. The observable economic facts belong to that phase and even such laws as we can derive from them are not applicable to other phases. Since the real purpose of socialism is precisely to overcome and advance beyond the predatory phase of human development, economic science in its present state can throw little light on the socialist society of the future.

Second, socialism is directed toward a social-ethical end. Science, however, cannot create ends and, even less, instill them in human beings; science, at most, can supply the means by which to attain certain ends. But the ends themselves are conceived by personalities with lofty ethical ideals and — if these ends are not stillborn, but vital and vigorous — are adopted and carried forward by those many human beings who, half unconsciously, determine the slow evolution of society.

For these reasons, we should be on our guard not to overestimate science and scientific methods when it is a question of human problems; and we should not assume that experts are the only ones who have a right to express themselves on questions affecting the organization of society.

Innumerable voices have been asserting for some time now that human society is passing through a crisis, that its stability has been gravely shattered. It is characteristic of such a situation that individuals feel indifferent or even hostile toward the group, small or large, to which they belong. In order to illustrate my meaning, let me record here a personal experience. I recently discussed with an intelligent and well-disposed man the threat of another war, which in my opinion would seriously endanger the existence of mankind, and I remarked that only a supranational organization would offer protection from that danger. Thereupon my visitor, very calmly and coolly, said to me: "Why are you so deeply opposed to the disappearance of the human race?"

I am sure that as little as a century ago no one would have so lightly made a statement of this kind. It is the statement of a man who has striven in vain to attain an equilibrium within himself and has more or less lost hope of succeeding. It is the expression of a painful solitude and isolation from which so many people are suffering in these days. What is the cause? Is there a way out?

It is easy to raise such questions, but difficult to answer them with any degree of assurance. I must try, however, as best I can, although I am very conscious of the fact that our feelings and strivings are often contradictory and obscure and that they cannot be expressed in easy and simple formulas.

Man is, at one and the same time, a solitary being and a social being. As a solitary being, he attempts to protect his own existence and that of those who are closest to him, to satisfy his personal desires, and to develop his innate abilities. As a social being, he seeks to gain the recognition and affection of his fellow human beings, to share in their pleasures, to comfort them in their sorrows, and to improve their conditions of life. Only the existence of these varied, frequently conflicting, strivings accounts for the special character of a man, and their specific combination determines the extent to which an individual can achieve an inner equilibrium and can contribute to the well-being of society. It is quite possible that the relative strength of these two drives is, in the main, fixed by inheritance. But the personality that finally emerges is largely formed by the environment in which a man happens to find himself during his development, by the structure of the society in which he grows up, by the tradition of that society, and by its appraisal of particular types of behavior. The abstract concept "society" means to the individual human being the sum total of his direct and indirect relations to his contemporaries and to all the people of earlier generations. The individual is able to think, feel, strive and work by himself; but he depends so much upon society — in his physical, intellectual and emotional existence — that it is impossible to think of him, or to understand him, outside the framework of society. It is "society" which provides man with food, clothing, a home, the tools of work, language, the forms of thought and most of the content of thought; his life is made possible through the labor and the accomplishments of the many millions past and present who are all hidden behind the small word "society."

It is evident, therefore, that the dependence of the individual upon society is a fact of nature which cannot be abolished — just as in the case of ants and bees. However, while the whole life process of ants and bees is fixed down to the smallest detail by rigid, hereditary instincts, the social pattern and interrelationships of human beings are very variable and susceptible to change. Memory, the capacity to make new combinations and the gift of oral communication have made possible developments among human beings which are not dictated by biological necessities. Such developments manifest themselves in traditions, institutions and organizations; in literature; in scientific and engineering accomplishments; in works of art. This explains how it happens that, in a certain sense, man can influence his life through his own conduct, and that in this process conscious thinking and wanting can play a part.

Man acquires at birth, through heredity, a biological constitution which we must consider fixed and unalterable, including the natural urges which are characteristic of the human species. In addition, during his lifetime, he acquires a cultural constitution which he adopts from society through communication and through many other types of influences. It is this cultural constitution which, with the passage of time, is subject to change and which determines to a very large extent the relationship between the individual and society. Modern anthropology has taught us, through comparative investigation of so-called primitive cultures, that the social behavior of human beings may differ greatly, depending upon prevailing cultural patterns and the types of organization which predominate in society. It is on this that those who are striving to improve the lot of man may ground their hopes: human beings are *not* condemned, because of their biological constitution, to annihilate each other or to be at the mercy of a cruel, self-inflicted fate.

If we ask ourselves how the structure of society and the cultural attitude of man should be changed in order to make human life as satisfying as possible, we should constantly be conscious of the fact that there are certain conditions which we are unable to modify. As mentioned before, the biological nature of man is, for all practical purposes, not subject to change. Furthermore, technological and demographic developments of the last few centuries have created conditions which are here to stay. In relatively densely settled populations with the goods which are indispensable to their continued existence, an extreme division of labor and a highly-centralized productive apparatus are absolutely necessary. The time — which, looking back, seems so idyllic — is gone forever when individuals or relatively small groups could be completely self-sufficient. It is only a slight exaggeration to say that mankind constitutes even now a planetary community of production and consumption.

I have now reached the point where I may indicate briefly what to me constitutes the essence of the crisis of our time. It concerns the relationship of the individual to society. The individual has become more conscious than ever of his dependence upon society. But he does not experience this dependence as a positive asset, as an organic tie, as a protective force, but rather as a threat to his natural rights, or even to his economic existence. Moreover, his position in society is such that the egotistical drives of his make-up are constantly being accentuated, while his social drives, which are by nature weaker, progressively deteriorate. All human beings, whatever their position in society, are suffering from this process of deterioration. Unknowingly prisoners of their own egotism, they feel insecure, lonely and deprived of the naive, simple and unsophisticated enjoyment of life. Man can find meaning in life, short and perilous as it is, only through devoting himself to society.

The economic anarchy of capitalist society as it exists today is, in my opinion, the real source of the evil. We see before us a huge community of producers the members of which are unceasingly striving to deprive each other of the fruits of their collective labor — not by force, but on the whole in faithful compliance with legally established rules. In this respect, it is important to realize that the means of production — that is to say, the entire productive capacity that is needed for producing consumer goods as well as additional capital goods — may legally be, and for the most part are, the private property of individuals.

For the sake of simplicity, in the discussion that follows I shall call "workers" all those who do not share in the ownership of the means of production — although this does not quite correspond to the customary use of the term. The owner of the means of production is in a position to purchase the labor power of the worker. By using the means of production, the worker produces new goods which become the property of the capitalist. The essential point about this process is the relation between what the worker produces and what he is paid, both measured in terms of real value. Insofar as the labor contract is "free," what the worker receives is determined not by the real value of the goods he produces, but by his minimum needs and by the capitalists' requirements for labor power in relation to the number of workers competing for jobs. It is important to understand that even in theory the payment of the worker is not determined by the value of his product.

Private capital tends to become concentrated in few hands, partly because of competition among the capitalists, and partly because technological development and the increasing division of labor encourage the formation of larger units of production at the expense of smaller ones. The result of these developments is an oligarchy of private capital the enormous power of which cannot be effectively checked even by a democratically organized political society. This is true since the members of legislative bodies are selected by political parties, largely financed or otherwise influenced by private capitalists who, for all practical purposes, separate the electorate from the legislature. The consequence is that the representatives of the people do not in fact sufficiently protect the interests of the underprivileged sections of the population. Moreover, under existing conditions, private capitalists inevitably control, directly or indirectly, the main sources of information (press, radio, education). It is thus extremely difficult, and indeed in most cases quite impossible, for the individual citizen to come to objective conclusions and to make intelligent use of his political rights.

The situation prevailing in an economy based on the private ownership of capital is thus characterized by two main principles: first, means of production (capital) are privately owned and the owners dispose of them as they see fit; second, the labor contract is free. Of course, there is no such thing as a *pure* capitalist society in this sense. In particular, it should be noted that the workers, through long and bitter political struggles, have succeeded in securing a somewhat improved form of the "free labor contract" for certain categories of workers. But taken as a whole, the present day economy does not differ much from "pure" capitalism.

Production is carried on for profit, not for use. There is no provision that all those able and willing to work will always be in a position to find employment; an "army of unemployed" almost always exists. The worker is constantly in fear of losing his job. Since unemployed and poorly paid workers do not provide a profitable market, the production of consumer goods is restricted, and great hardship is the consequence. Technological progress frequently results in more unemployment rather than in an easing of the burden of work for all. The profit motive, in conjunction with competition among capitalists, is responsible for an instability in the accumulation and utilization of capital which leads to increasingly severe depressions. Unlimited competition leads to a huge waste of labor, and to that crippling of the social consciousness of individuals which I mentioned before.

This crippling of individuals I consider the worst evil of capitalism. Our whole educational system suffers from this evil. An exaggerated competitive attitude is inculcated into the student, who is trained to worship acquisitive success as a preparation for his future career.

I am convinced there is only *one* way to eliminate these grave evils, namely through the establishment of a socialist economy, accompanied by an educational system which would be oriented toward social goals. In such an economy, the means of production are owned by society itself and are utilized in a planned fashion. A planned economy, which adjusts production to the needs of the community, would distribute the work to be done among all those able to work and would guarantee a livelihood to every man, woman and child. The education of the individual, in addition to promoting his own innate abilities, would attempt to develop in him a sense of responsibility for his fellow men in place of the glorification of power and success in our present society.

Nevertheless, it is necessary to remember that a planned economy is not yet socialism. A planned economy as such may be accompanied by the complete enslavement of the individual. The achievement of socialism requires the solution of some extremely difficult sociopolitical problems: how is it possible, in view of the far-reaching centralization of political and economic power, to prevent bureaucracy from becoming all-powerful and overweening? How can the rights of the individual be protected and therewith a democratic counterweight to the power of bureaucracy be assured?

Clarity about the aims and problems of socialism is of greatest significance in our age of transition. Since, under present circumstances, free and unhindered discussion of these problems has come under a powerful taboo, I consider the foundation of this magazine [*Monthly Review*] to be an important public service.

(1949)

Thoughts on the World Economic Crisis

If there is anything that can give a layman in the sphere of economics the courage to express an opinion on the nature of the alarming economic difficulties of the present day, it is the hopeless confusion of opinions among the experts. What I have to say is nothing new and does not pretend to be anything more than the expression of the opinion of an independent and honest man who, unburdened by class or national prejudices, desires nothing but the good of humanity and the most harmonious possible scheme of human existence. If in what follows I write as if I were sure of the truth of what I am saying, this is merely done for the sake of an easier mode of expression; it does not proceed from unwarranted self-confidence or a belief in the infallibility of my somewhat simple intellectual conception of problems which are in reality uncommonly complex.

As I see it, this crisis differs in character from past crises in that it is based on an entirely new set of conditions, arising out of the rapid progress in methods of production. Only a fraction of the available human labor in the world is now needed for the production of the total amount of consumption goods necessary to life. Under a completely laissez-faire economic system, this fact is bound to lead to unemployment.

For reasons which I do not propose to analyze here, the majority of people are compelled to work for the minimum wage on which life can be supported. If two factories produce the same sort of goods, other things being equal, that factory will be able to produce them more cheaply which employs fewer workmen — i.e., makes the individual worker work as long and as hard as human nature permits. From this it follows inevitably that, with methods of production as they are today, only a portion of the available labor can be used. While unreasonable demands are made on this portion, the remainder is automatically excluded from the process of production. This leads to a fall in sales and profits. Businesses go smash, which further increases unemployment and diminishes confidence in industrial concerns and therewith public participation in the mediating banks; finally the banks become insolvent through the sudden withdrawal of accounts and the wheels of industry therewith come to a complete standstill.

The crisis has also been attributed to other causes which we will now consider.

Over-production. We have to distinguish between two things here — real over-production and apparent over-production. By real over-production I mean a production so great that it exceeds the demand. This may perhaps apply to motor cars and wheat in the United States at the present moment, although even that is doubtful. By "over-production" people usually mean a condition in which more of one particular article is produced than can, in existing circumstances, be sold, in spite of a shortage of consumption goods among consumers. This I call apparent over-production. In this case it is not the demand that is lacking but the consumers' purchasing power. Such apparent over-production is only another word for a crisis and therefore cannot serve as an explanation of the latter; hence people who try to make over-production responsible for the present crisis are merely juggling with words.

Reparations. The obligation to pay reparations lies heavy on the debtor nations and their economies. It compels them to go in for dumping and so harms the creditor nations too. This is beyond dispute. But the appearance of the crisis in the United States, in spite of the high tariff-wall, proves that this cannot be the principal cause of the world crisis. The shortage of gold in the debtor countries due to reparations can at most serve as an argument for putting an end to these payments; it cannot provide an explanation of the world crisis.

Erection of new tariff-walls. Increase in the unproductive burden of armaments. Political insecurity owing to latent danger of war. All these things make the situation in Europe considerably worse without really affecting the United States. The appearance of the crisis in the United States shows that they cannot be its principal causes.

The dropping-out of the two powers, China and Russia. Also this blow to world trade cannot make itself very deeply felt in the United States and therefore cannot be the principal cause of the crisis.

The economic rise of the lower classes since the war. This, supposing it to be a reality, could only produce a scarcity of goods, not an excessive supply.

I will not weary the reader by enumerating further contentions which do not seem to me to get to the heart of the matter. Of one thing I feel certain: this same technical progress which, in itself, might relieve mankind of a great part of the labor necessary to its subsistence, is the main cause of our present misery. Hence there are those who would in all seriousness forbid the introduction of technical improvements. This is obviously absurd. But how can we find a more rational way out of our dilemma?

If we could somehow manage to prevent the purchasing power

of the masses, measured in terms of goods, from sinking below a certain minimum, stoppages in the industrial cycle such as we are experiencing today would be rendered impossible.

The logically simplest but also most daring method of achieving this is a completely planned economy, in which consumption goods are produced and distributed by the community. That is essentially what is being attempted in Russia today. Much will depend on what results this forced experiment produces. To hazard a prophecy here would be presumption. Can goods be produced as economically under such a system as under one which leaves more freedom to individual enterprise? Can this system maintain itself at all without the terror that has so far accompanied it, to which none of us westerners would care to expose himself? Does not such a rigid, centralized economic system tend toward protectionism and toward resistance to advantageous innovations? We must take care, however, not to allow these misgivings to become prejudices which prevent us from forming an objective judgment.

My personal opinion is that those methods are in general preferable which respect existing traditions and habits so far as that is in any way compatible with the end in view. Nor do I believe that a sudden transference of economy into governmental management would be beneficial from the point of view of production; private enterprise should be left its sphere of activity, insofar as it has not already been eliminated by industry itself by the [devices of cartels].

There are, however, two respects in which this economic freedom ought to be limited. In each branch of industry the number of working hours per week ought so to be reduced by law that unemployment is systematically abolished. At the same time minimum wages must be fixed in such a way that the purchasing power of the workers keeps pace with production.

Further, in those industries which have become monopolistic in character through organization on the part of the producers, prices must be controlled by the state in order to keep the issue of capital within reasonable bounds and prevent the artificial strangling of production and consumption.

In this way it might perhaps be possible to establish a proper balance between production and consumption without too great a limitation of free enterprise and at the same time to stop the intolerable tyranny of the owners of the means of production (land and machinery) over the wage earners, in the widest sense of the term.

(Published in 1934)

On Wealth

I am absolutely convinced that no wealth in the world can help humanity forward, even in the hands of the most devoted worker in this cause. The example of great and pure individuals is the only thing that can lead us to noble thoughts and deeds. Money only appeals to selfishness and irresistibly invites abuse. Can anyone imagine Moses, Jesus or Gandhi armed with the money-bags of Carnegie?

(Published in 1934)

Science and Society

There are two ways in which science affects human affairs. The first is familiar to everyone: Directly, and to an even greater extent indirectly, science produces aids that have completely transformed human existence. The second way is educational in character — it works on the mind. Although it may appear less obvious to cursory examination, it is no less incisive than the first.

The most conspicuous practical effect of science is that it

makes possible the contriving of things that enrich life, though they complicate it at the same time — inventions such as the steam engine, the railway, electric power and light, the telegraph, radio, automobile, airplane, dynamite, etc. To these must be added the life-preserving achievements of biology and medicine, especially the production of pain relievers and preservative methods of storing food. The greatest practical benefit which all these inventions confer on man I see in the fact that they liberate him from the excessive muscular drudgery that was once indispensable for the preservation of bare existence. Insofar as we may at all claim that slavery has been abolished today, we owe its abolition to the practical consequences of science.

On the other hand, technology — or applied science — has confronted mankind with problems of profound gravity. The very survival of mankind depends on a satisfactory solution of these problems. It is a matter of creating the kind of social institutions and traditions without which the new tools must inevitably bring disaster of the worst kind.

Mechanical means of production in an unorganized economy have had the result that a substantial proportion of mankind is no longer needed for the production of goods and is thus excluded from the process of economic circulation. The immediate consequences are the weakening of purchasing power and the devaluation of labor because of excessive competition, and these give rise, at ever shortening intervals, to a grave paralysis in the production of goods. Ownership of the means of production, on the other hand, carries a power to which the traditional safeguards of our political institutions are unequal. Mankind is caught up in a struggle for adaptation to these new conditions — a struggle that may bring true liberation, if our generation shows itself equal to the task.

Technology has also shortened distances and created new and extraordinarily effective means of destruction which, in the hands of nations claiming unrestricted freedom of action, become threats to the security and very survival of mankind. This situation requires a single judicial and executive power for the entire planet, and the creation of such a central authority is desperately opposed by national traditions. Here too we are in the midst of a struggle whose issue will decide the fate of all of us.

Means of communication, finally — reproduction processes for the printed word, and the radio — when combined with modern weapons, have made it possible to place body and soul under bondage to a central authority — and here is a third source of danger to mankind. Modern tyrannies and their destructive effects show plainly how far we are from exploiting these achievements organizationally for the benefit of mankind. Here too circumstances require an international solution, with the psychological foundation for such a solution not yet laid.

Let us now turn to the intellectual effects that proceed from science. In prescientific times it was not possible by means of thought alone to attain results that all mankind could have accepted as certain and necessary. Still less was there a conviction that all that happens in nature is subject to inexorable laws. The fragmentary character of natural law, as seen by the primitive observer, was such as to foster a belief in ghosts and spirits. Hence even today primitive man lives in constant fear that supernatural and arbitrary forces will intervene in his destiny.

It stands to the everlasting credit of science that by acting on the human mind it has overcome man's insecurity before himself and before nature. In creating elementary mathematics the Greeks for the first time wrought a system of thought whose conclusions no one could escape. The scientists of the Renaissance then devised the combination of systematic experiment with mathematical method. This union made possible such precision in the formulation of natural laws and such certainty in checking them by experience that as a result there was no longer room for basic differences of opinion in natural science. Since that time each generation has built up the heritage of knowledge and understanding, without the slightest danger of a crisis that might jeopardize the whole structure.

The general public may be able to follow the details of scientific research to only a modest degree; but it can register at least one great and important gain: confidence that human thought is dependable and natural law universal.

(Published in 1935-36)

RESOURCES

Web

Einstein's FBI files: **www.foia.fbi.gov/einstein.htm**

Albert Einstein Archives at the Jewish National and University Library at the Hebrew University in Jerusalem: **www.albert-einstein.org**

Albert Einstein Online: **www.westegg.com/einstein**

Albert Einstein Library: **www.geocities.com/einstein_library/index.htm**

American Institute of Physics: **www.aip.org/history/einstein**

Print Media

Albert Einstein, *Ideas and Opinions*, New York: Modern Library, 1994 (first published in 1954)

Albert Einstein, *The World As I See It*, New York: Citadel Press, 1991 (first published in 1935)

Albert Einstein, *Out of My Later Years*, New York: Wings Books, 1996 (first edition 1950)

Albert Einstein and Sigmund Freud, *Why War?*, International Institute of Intellectual Cooperation, League of Nations, 1933

Fred Jerome, *The Einstein File: J. Edgar Hoover's Secret War Against the World's Most Famous Scientist*, New York: St. Martin's Press, 2002

Helen Dukas and Banesh Hoffman, *Albert Einstein, the Human Side: New Glimpses from his Archives*, Princeton, N.J.: Princeton University Press, 1979

rebel lives

haydée santamaría
edited by Betsy Maclean

"Haydée Santamaría signifies a
world, an attitude, a sensibility as
well as a revolution."
— *Mario Benedetti*

Haydée first achieved notoriety by
being one of two women who
participated in the armed attack
that sparked the Cuban
Revolution. Later, as director of
the world-renowned literary
institution, Casa de las Américas,
she embraced culture as a tool for
social change and provided refuge
for exiled Latin American artists
and intellectuals.

**Includes reflections by Ariel
Dorfman, Mario Benedetti,
Alicia Alonso and
Silvio Rodríguez.**

ISBN 1-876175-59-1 / US$11.95

helen keller
edited by John Davis

"I have entered the fight against
the economic system in which we
live. It is to be a fight to the
finish and I ask no quarter."
— *Helen Keller*

Poor little blind girl or dangerous
radical? This book challenges the
sanitized image of Helen Keller,
restoring her true history as a
militant socialist. Here are her
views on women's suffrage, her
defense of the Industrial
Workers of the World (IWW),
her opposition to World War I
and her support for imprisoned
socialist and anarchist leaders, as
well as her analysis of disability
and class.

ISBN 1-876175-60-5 / US$9.95

oceanpress

e-mail info@oceanbooks.com.au
www.oceanbooks.com.au